BIRDWATCHING WALKS
IN THE YORKSHIRE DALES

Birdwatching Walks
in the
Yorkshire Dales

Brendan Threlfall

Drawings by Milan Ivanič and Suzanna Ivanič

Palatine Books

This project is part funded by the Yorkshire Dales National Park Authority's Sustainable Development Fund, which is managed by the Yorkshire Dales Millennium Trust.

YORKSHIRE DALES
National Park Authority

YORKSHIRE DALES
MILLENNIUM TRUST

First published in the UK in 2008 by
Palatine Books
an imprint of Carnegie Publishing Ltd,
Carnegie House,
Chatsworth Road,
Lancaster LA1 4SL
www.palatinebooks.com

Cataloguing-in-Publication data
A catalogue record for this book is available from the British Library

ISBN 13: 978-1-874181-53-8
Typeset by Carnegie Book Production, Lancaster
Printed and bound in the UK by Alden Press, Witney

Contents

Dentdale, Garsdale and the Howgills

Wensleydale, Swaledale and Arkengarthdale

Foreword

THE YORKSHIRE DALES NATIONAL PARK AUTHORITY is delighted to be supporting the publication of this book on the birds of the Yorkshire Dales through its Sustainable Development Fund.

It may seem strange at first that such a fund devoted to promoting ways of living sustainably in the countryside is being used for this book, but birds are some of our most sensitive indicators of climate change. Here at the National Park Authority we take the threat of climate change very seriously. If it continues unchecked many of the habitats and species that make this National Park so special may be lost forever.

Take the red grouse, for instance. Walk across heather moorland in the Yorkshire Dales and you are bound to see red grouse diving low across the heather or sitting on a wall making that distinctive laughing 'go-back' noise. This bird lives in a fine balance with the cool, damp, windswept hills of the Dales. Research by the RSPB has shown that the red grouse are already disappearing from their most southerly ranges as the weather patterns warm and change. They predict that by 2075 suitable climate will restrict the grouse to the Scottish Highlands.

We may lose birds like the red grouse but a warming climate will bring new species to the National Park, hitherto restricted to the southern parts of Britain. If suitable habitats are not available for these new arrivals, however, they will not survive.

The National Park Authority is already aware that we need to encourage land managers to create habitat corridors or stepping stones for these potential new species as they travel north.

To find out more about the wonderful diversity of wildlife in the Yorkshire Dales National Park and what we are doing to conserve it for the future please visit the 'Nature in The Dales' pages on our website www.yorkshire dales.org.uk.

This of course assumes that climate change will continue unchecked. As visitors to the Yorkshire Dales National Park we can all do our bit to be greener and help mitigate the effects our visit has on the environment. Perhaps the most important is to reduce your carbon footprint by giving your car a holiday too! The Yorkshire Dales and its wildlife are best appreciated at a slower pace anyway, so walk, cycle or use public transport to get about. You'll avoid the hassle of parking your car and the stress of driving on narrow roads. You'll also ease pollution and pressure on the narrow Dales roads and limited car parks. Shopping in Dales' village shops rather than bringing your supplies with you and staying overnight rather than coming for a day visit helps the local economy, maintains jobs and improves the quality of life for local people.

We hope that you enjoy this book and will be inspired to come and view some of the birds described for yourselves. If you do, remember to be a green visitor and work with us to create a sustainable future for coming generations of residents and visitors.

Karen Griffiths
Communications Manager
Yorkshire Dales National Park Authority
10 September 2008

Acknowledgments

THE FOLLOWING PEOPLE have been instrumental in assisting me with this book and I would like to thank them wholeheartedly for all their help: Milan Ivanič for his excellent depictions of the star Dales species; Ian Court generously gave his time and advice in the early stages; Tony Vittery was a source of encouragment and local sightings throughout and kindly read through draft accounts of several walks; Ian Robert Smithson, whose knowledge of the flora and history of Swaledale and Tan Hill was exemplary and illuminating; Christine Threlfall made excellent company on several walks and has a navigational ability second to none; Maggie Gallagher provided much appreciated food and advice; Graham Threlfall without whom I would not have this fantastic hobby; Roz Ivanič who was hugely helpful and supportive as ever; and last but not least Suzanna Ivanič, chief enthusiast and walking partner, very able support artist and highly entertaining bird identifier!

Introduction

THE YORKSHIRE DALES IS an enchantingly beautiful area of the central Pennines in the heart of northern England. It is an area of limestone pavements and scars, fast flowing rivers and waterfalls, lonely heather moors and picturesque villages and valleys. Interpretations of 'The Yorkshire Dales' vary but this book will use the National Park boundary along with Upper Nidderdale north of Pateley Bridge. Three sites that lie just outside these boundaries are included because they are very close to the National Park and each offers something different and exciting to the birdwatcher.

Much has been written on walking in the Dales but the birds of this special area remain comparatively uncelebrated. Hopefully this book will encourage people to explore an area that is excellent for birds regardless of the experience of the observer. The beginner might be happy to marvel at the dippers at Aysgarth or a great spotted woodpecker in Grass Woods but the experienced birder will still find much here to attract them. The Dales are home to the most southerly population of black grouse in the country and scarce breeding birds like wood warbler, pied flycatcher and nightjar. With dotterels stopping off on migration, there is plenty to satisfy even the keenest birdwatcher.

This book is part of a series which promotes a 'Birdwatching walks' concept. This idea has much to commend it. Modern site guides for birders can create a 'drive up and tick' mentality where well-known sites are visited by car. There is no substitute, though, for leaving the car behind and having a good walk in the gorgeous Dales. Walking of course increases your chance of seeing many birds that don't lend themselves to the drive and tick idea, such as birds of prey. Within each walk, certain areas have been specified as good places to stop and search more thoroughly for birds. The amount of birdwatching done within the walk is up to you. This guide can help with a family trip to Aysgarth where you sneak a bit of birdwatching in or a more thorough search of Strid Woods for wood warbler and pied flycatcher. The more time you give to stopping to actively seek out the birds, the more you will see, particularly in woodlands or at areas of water like Hellifield Flash. You should bear this in mind when considering the warning about the estimates given for the walk duration.

Each walk has a particular theme based mostly on a target bird. Look carefully at the time of year and habitat suggested for the star bird to maximise your chances. It is important to remember, though, that luck will always play its part. All the sites given for certain species are known to be good at the time of writing but things change and birds can be unpredictable. The best advice if you are really determined would be to be thorough and persistent. With a few days non-stop birding planned in the prime time of early May 2007 I nearly found my efforts scuppered by awful weather. For three days I saw little and got a thorough soaking for my troubles. Plans for a trip to the northern Dales sadly had to be abandoned. Thankfully I narrowly resisted the temptation to abandon birding altogether for the week and headed off to Grass Woods when the rain had eased a little. Within half an hour wood warbler, pied flycatcher, tree pipit and peregrine had cheered me up immensely and my luck continued when a hike up Ingleborough that afternoon rewarded me with a stunning 'trip' of 11 dotterel on the summit!

One of the advantages of the book will be that, even if you don't have much luck with the birds, the walks are fantastic in their own right. Take waterfalls for example: this book includes England's highest overall, England's highest above ground, England's highest single drop, and the rightly popular series at Aysgarth and Ingleton. With a supporting cast of Hell Gill Force, Kisdon Force, Posforth Force, Linton Falls, Janet's Foss, Kisdon Force and Catrake Force, birdwatching can be combined with admiring many much-loved water-falls. When it came to selection, if two walks were felt to have similar birds the one with the better scenery was included.

In order to protect the locations of some rare and persecuted breeding birds (hen harrier and goshawk particularly) some sites in the Dales have been omitted from this guide. Where the risk was felt to be lower and the sites were already extremely widely known, it was felt safe to include them (for example, black grouse at Arkengarthdale, peregrines at Malham, nightjars at Timble etc.) Even with the much persecuted hen harrier, thinking in conservation circles is beginning to turn towards mobilising birdwatchers and the public to help protect this beleaguered raptor. Empty moors only help those who would threaten the harriers. Even so it is best to err on the side of caution and it is hoped a fair balance has been struck here. Nest sites have, of course, not been included and walkers should take special care not to disturb scarce breeding birds. Disturbing Schedule 1 breeding species (which include kingfisher and little ringed plover) is a serious offence under the Wildlife and Countryside Act. Those wishing to photograph Schedule 1 species at or near the nest must apply for a license. The Code of Conduct for viewing black grouse has been printed in full here and should also be diligently observed by birdwatchers.

Code of Conduct for viewing black grouse

1. Avoid looking for black grouse after heavy snowfalls, when birds are under stress.
2. View leks from a vehicle. Black grouse pay little attention to stationary vehicles that are at least 100 metres away. Ensure that you do not block access and that your presence will not disturb nearby residents. Avoid approaching a lek on foot, which usually disturbs the birds.
3. Arrive before daybreak. A vehicle stopping once it is light can disturb the birds. Stay in your vehicle and watch quietly through binoculars and telescopes. Get the flask of coffee from the boot before your vigil! Don't start the engine until after lekking has wound down, usually about two hours after dawn. Alternatively, consider watching a lek in the evening.
4. Keep to footpaths, especially in June and July, when there may be nesting females and young birds present. Do not go looking for black grouse in heather or thick field vegetation, especially in woodland as birds may fly into deer fences, with lethal consequences, if flushed.
5. Do not bring dogs into the field when you're watching grouse.

How to use this book

Walk directions and safety

Detailed directions and a sketch map are included for each walk but you should also take an Ordnance Survey map with you. Ideally take one of the Outdoor Leisure Series – numbers 2, 19 and 30 cover the area used in this book (Yorkshire Dales Southern and Western, Howgill Fells and Upper Eden Valley, and Yorkshire Dales Northern and Central). Hopefully the directions given will prove useful but it is worth pointing out that signposts can fall down and paths be rerouted or disappear. Common sense, a compass and a keen eye on the detail of the map are all still highly recommended, particularly on the longer walks over higher ground.

When walking on the fells always remember the other crucial basics – warm clothing, food and drink, a good pair of walking boots and a mobile phone if you have one. It is still best to let someone know where you are going because you cannot get mobile phone reception in many parts of the Dales. In winter be particularly prepared and check the weather forecast beforehand to try and avoid days when heavy mist and fog descend on the tops.

Timing

A rough estimate of the time needed to complete the walk has been included. This needs a particular note of caution, however, as it is inevitably a subjective estimate. The estimate is based on a slow birdwatching pace but some will find this too cautious. Others will stop to soak in the birds and views and find a 2 to 3 hour walk can take the best part of a day. Be aware of your own pace and try to allow more time than you might need.

Countryside Code

Be safe – plan ahead and follow any signs

Leave gates and property as you find them

Protect plants and animals, and take your litter home

Keep dogs under close control

Consider other people

More information on the countryside code can be found at www.countrysideaccess.gov.uk

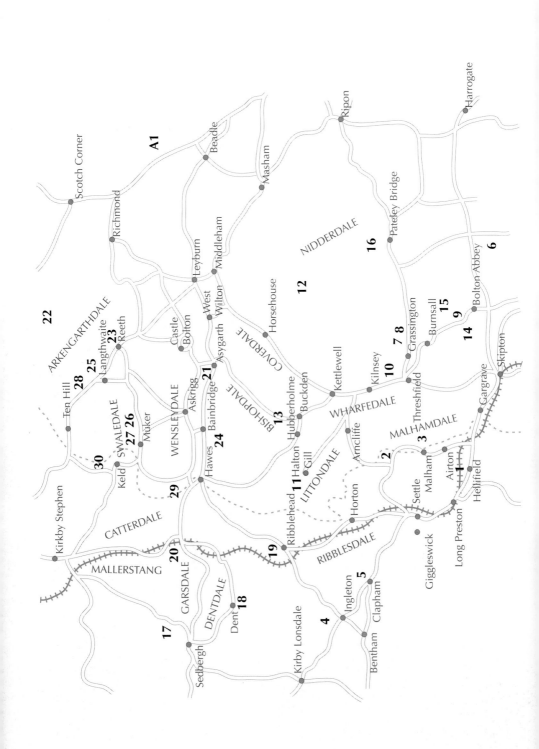

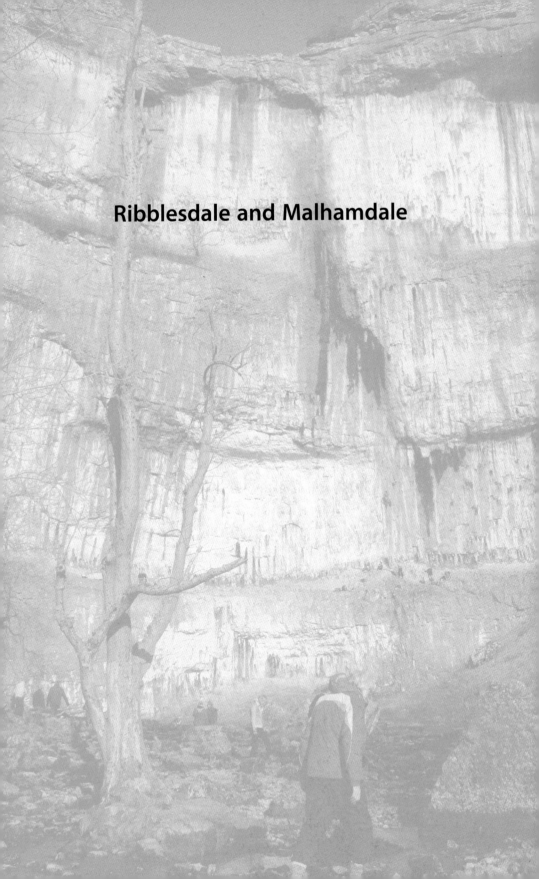

Ribblesdale and Malhamdale

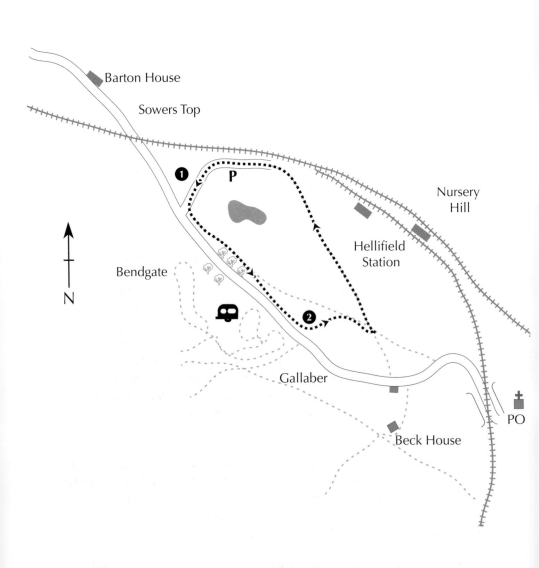

Barton House

Sowers Top

P

Nursery
Hill

Hellifield
Station

Bendgate

Gallaber

Beck House

PO

N

Hellifield

Refuge for migrants at Hellifield

Black-tailed godwit

Length: 2 km (1.25 miles)

Time: Allow 1 hour

Season: All year, late April to early June and August/
September are best for migrant waders
(though this depends to a large extent on
water levels).

Terrain/grade: Easy

Start: Layby on Waterside Lane off the A65 near
Hellifield village. You can park anywhere along
the lane as it is usually very quiet, SD844574

Bus/train: Hellifield railway station provides easy access
to the flash and is served by trains running on
the Leeds to Morecambe and Leeds to Carlisle
routes. Pennine runs the 580 bus service
between Skipton and Settle that stops at the
Black Horse in Hellifield (Monday to Saturday).

General: Refreshments in Hellifield village

THIS SHORT WALK AROUND Hellifield Flash is packed with excitement for
the birdwatcher at any time of the year. If mud is exposed in the spring
or autumn, the flash is a haven for migrant waders. A number of records of
scarce and rare birds here have attracted twitchers from across the county.
This is the walk for those who delight in anticipating the unexpected.

❶ **From the layby head along Waterside Lane towards the A65.
Turn left at the junction and walk along the grassy verge for a
short distance before taking the path through the small wooden
gate on your left. Follow the path through the young plantation
and follow it round to the right as it skirts the edge of the road.**

❶ The autumn and winter months at the flash are dominated by wildfowl, with several hundred wigeon often present. Teal feed in the margins and shovelers resurface after upending to reveal their huge bills. The beautifully elegant pintail is a real draw in the winter months, with double figures of this duck sometimes seen. Diving ducks are present in lower numbers though tufted duck and pochard can normally be found. The attractive white plumage of the male goldeneye is often on show and the compact little grebe is present throughout the winter. The rare grey phalarope has been seen here on several occasions in late autumn after heavy gales have blown them in from the coast. Grey herons fly lazily over the flash and the winter months can see occasional parties of pink-footed goose or whooper swan stopping off.

(⚘) **❷ You come to a wooden gate where you need to turn left and through another gate. Head over the field at around 1 o'clock towards a metal gate and a small footbridge over the stream. Bear left after this and pick up the path heading back towards Waterside Lane. Head over the stile and turn left onto the lane to return to the layby.**

❶ It is during the migration periods that the flash really comes into its own as a place to look for scarce visitors to the Dales. Hellifield's position in the Ribble Valley means it acts as a stop-off point for birds migrating west or east along the valley. Late April to early June has been best for birdwatching in the past few years as the high winter water levels have dropped to expose the mud favoured by passage waders. Black-tailed godwit often pass through in mid to late April on their way to breeding grounds in Iceland. They are a stunning bird with their deep orange summer plumage. They can be distinguished from the similar bar-tailed godwit by their longer, straighter bill and long tibiae (length of leg above the knee). Dunlin, ringed plover and common sandpiper are expected during the spring wader passage and join the little ringed plovers that arrive first and breed here. Rarer waders have been recorded here in spring with recent sightings including wood sandpiper and little stint. Late April also sees yellow wagtails pass through, whilst the flash is a reliable spring site for seeing white wagtails. The white wagtail is a type of pied wagtail which can be distinguished easily in spring by its silvery grey, as opposed to black, upperparts.

If a long period of dry weather has dried the flash out the summer months can be a non-event at Hellifield, but if there is water a good selection of birds can still be seen. Lapwing numbers build up towards late summer as birds disperse from their Dales breeding haunts. The little ringed plovers usually remain, depending on water levels. Their sandy plumage is a perfect camouflage in the rocky areas at the water's edge. The late summer has, a little surprisingly, proved productive for birds of prey at Hellifield recently. Peregrines dispersing from nearby breeding areas (Walk 3) have made regular appearances and other notable records have included hobby and goshawk. When all the lapwing take flight and alarm call, be alert for a raptor, though it might be a stoat or the farmer that is panicking them.

Little ringed plover

Autumn may see many lamenting the passing of summer but for birdwatchers it can be the most exciting time of the year. Water levels at Hellifield are key, but if there is mud the birdwatcher can expect a few ruff around the edges or mixing with the lapwing. Wood sandpiper has been recorded here in autumn. This smart wader breeds mainly in Scandinavia and Russia and migrants seen in Britain are tracking down to wintering grounds south of the Sahara Desert. If you are lucky enough to see a wood sandpiper, expect it to be feeding vigorously as it has a long way left to go in its remarkable journey. Garganeys are in a similar position; in their case the destination is West Africa where they will form flocks several-hundred-thousand strong at favoured sites in Cameroon, Mali and Senegal. Look for garganey in September when teal numbers increase. Check carefully because they are not easy to pick out at this time of year. Even the males are in an eclipse plumage similar to the subtle females to help protect them from predation as they moult their feathers. Look for a duck with a more prominent head pattern than the teal, formed by a broad supercilium (stripe above the eye), and a pale spot at the base of the bill. Dales birdwatching normally revolves around appreciation of the wonderful residents and breeding species but the beauty of this walk lies in the chance of something different and unpredictable. Good luck!

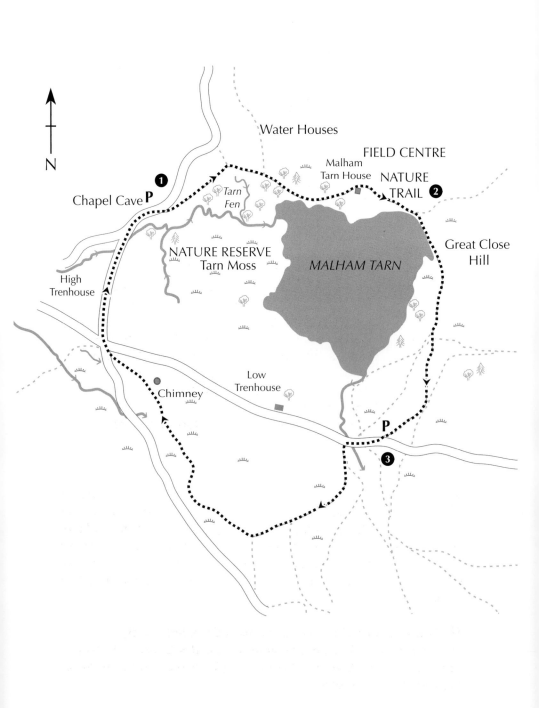

N

Water Houses

FIELD CENTRE

Malham
Tarn House

NATURE
TRAIL ❷

Chapel Cave **P** ❶

*Tarn
Fen*

Great Close
Hill

NATURE RESERVE
Tarn Moss

MALHAM TARN

High
Trenhouse

Chimney

Low
Trenhouse

P

❸

Malham Tarn

Birds and butterflies around Malham Tarn

Dark green fritillary

Length:	6 km (3.5 miles)
Time:	2 to 3 hours
Season:	All year
Terrain/grade:	Easy
Start:	Free car park to the west of Malham Tarn in the small disused quarry, SD882672. An alternative starting point is at the National Trust car park at the southern end of the tarn (see map opposite)
Bus/train:	Nearest buses run to Malham village except a minibus shuttle service on weekends and Bank Holidays which runs from Settle and stops at the tarn. This service runs between April and September (funding dependent)
General:	Nearest refreshments and toilets at Malham village

MALHAM TARN HAS A wonderful location, set amidst limestone scars and pavements in an area famed for its scenery. One of only two natural lakes in the Dales (Semer Water, walk 24, is the other) the tarn is a haven for ducks in the winter. The fen on its western shore is home to numerous butterflies and dragonflies in the summer. With a not too strenuous walk and a wealth of wildlife on show, a visit to this area should require little encouragement.

❶ **Turn right out of the car park and take a left shortly afterwards through a wooden gate. Follow this track, with Tarn Fen over to your right, and then turn right at the junction to head towards the field centre.**

❶ Malham Tarn is such a good place for all kinds of wildlife that it is difficult to focus solely on birds. Those interested in butterflies will find plenty to keep them busy here, with the scarce green hairstreak and dark green fritillary both present on Tarn Fen. You can obtain a permit for a small fee from the estate office or field studies centre to allow you to walk along the boardwalk across the fen. The dark green fritillary can be seen on Tarn Fen from the second week of July to around the first week of September. Green hairstreaks are easy to identify thanks to their green underwing, though this can appear almost turquoise in colour at some angles. They are on the wing in May and June. With small and large skipper, numerous green-veined whites and occasional commas also on show, the area is a real treat for the butterfly enthusiast.

In addition to the butterflies, there are plenty of dragonflies on the fen, with August a particularly good month to see them. Emerald, azure and common blue damselflies can be seen and black darters are numerous by the end of the month.

It would be a mistake to neglect the birdlife of Malham Tarn, however, with interesting sightings possible at any time of year. Look from the track skirting the fen for redpoll and check the area around Keeper's Cottage for spotted flycatcher. The bird hide on your right past the cottage is worth spending some time in and gives a good view out over the tarn. Little and great crested grebes can be seen from here throughout the year. In summer plumage they are a particularly attractive duo and might be on show close into the hide if you are lucky. The Reverend Peake wrote an account of the birds of the area way back in the late-nineteenth century and specifically mentioned the little grebes on the tarn. 'Out on Malham Tarn,' the Reverend observed, 'this bird does not behave with its usual shyness, and its ways and noises may be easily observed.' Over 110 years later the same is still true, though thanks to the hide and improved optics the views of this charming species are even better now.

The tarn is not really suited to attracting passage waders, though an occasional greenshank or ruff might be seen. The spring and autumn passage periods can produce a surprise like a black tern or osprey, but the winter months are best for the number of birds on the tarn itself. Tufted duck, mallard, teal and coot are present throughout the year but in the winter months they are complemented by over a hundred wigeon and several hundred pochard. A few dozen handsome goldeneye winter and make a fine sight on a crisp January morning.

Ⓚ ❷ **At the field studies centre bear left and then right to walk around the back of the centre and pick up the path heading through the woods. Out of the woods bear right on the Pennine Way. You can either keep on this to the road or bear right along the wall to Tarn Foot and join the road here.**

ⓘ Moving into Tarn Woods check for redstart and spotted flycatcher in spring and summer before leaving the woods at the north-eastern edge of the tarn. Great Close Scar on your left is worth investigation at any time of year. Peregrines are regularly seen here in the winter and raven should always be looked for. Spring and summer sees the charming wheatear perch boldly on scattered rocks, whilst April can be a good month to see ring ouzel.

Ⓚ ❸ **Turn right onto the road, head through the gate and then take a left soon after. Bear right uphill on the grassy bridleway signed to Langscar Gate. Ignore the left turning to Malham and continue to a gap in the wall. Here you need to leave the stony track and bear right at about 2 o'clock to a wooden post visible up the hill. From this post bear right very slightly to take you to a small stile in the wall opposite. In the next field keep close to the wall on your right and then head straight at the next marker post. Soon you need to bear right towards a small marker post in the front of the chimney. At the chimney the path virtually disappears but head left to the corner of the field by the crossroads. Once on the road head straight on signed to Arncliffe and then bear right at the next junction. Follow the road back to the car park.**

ⓘ As you continue along the road towards Low Trenhouse, look for one of our most eye-catching summer visitors, the stunning yellow wagtail. They are complemented here by attractive breeding waders including lapwing, redshank, common sandpiper and oystercatcher. The walk back over the fields keeps the birdwatcher entertained with wheatears on the limestone pavement and curlews in the fields by the chimney. Be sure to check Tarn Moss from the road. In winter you might have the pleasure here of watching a hen harrier quartering the raised bog.

Yellow wagtail

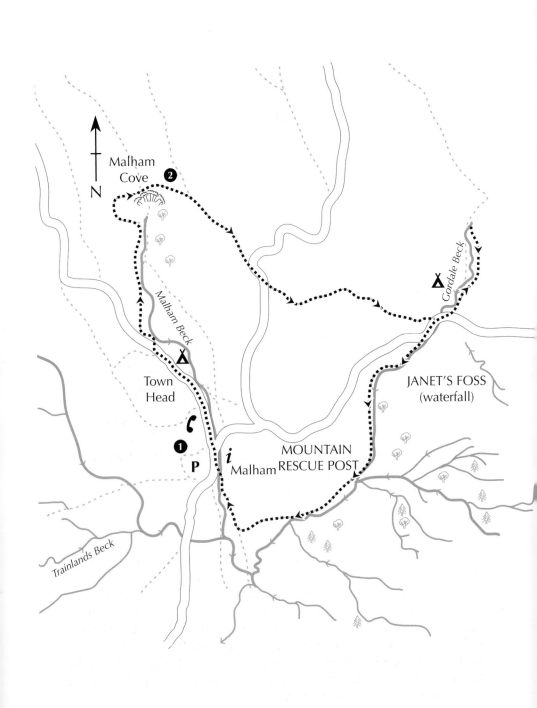

N

Malham
Cove **2**

Malham Beck

Gordale Beck

Town
Head

JANET'S FOSS
(waterfall)

1

P

i Malham

MOUNTAIN
RESCUE POST

Trainlands Beck

Malham Cove

Peregrines at Malham Cove

Peregrine

Length: 6.5 km (4 miles)

Time: Around 3 hours

Season: Late March to late July (note that the area can become very crowded with tourists on summer weekends and bank holidays)

Terrain/grade: Moderate

Start: Malham YDNP car park, SD901627

Bus/train: The 210 Monday to Saturday service runs between Malham and Skipton, stopping at the Buck Inn in Malham. There is currently a minibus shuttle service on weekends and Bank Holidays, which runs between Settle and Malham National Parks centre (April to September – funding dependent). There is also a limited Dales Experience bus, which runs on selected Summer Sundays from West Yorkshire to Malham

General: Refreshments and toilets in Malham. There is sometimes a snack van at Gordale

THIS WALK COMBINES SOME of the most impressive limestone scenery in the Dales with the likelihood of seeing the fast and powerful peregrine falcon. A pair of peregrines nests every year on Malham Cove, which stands at around 80 metres high and 300 metres wide. An RSPB watchpoint has been established to show visitors the birds and this is manned from early April until the end of July (contact Malham National Park Centre for further details). Add the formidable presence of the cove to the ravine of Gordale Scar and the more gentle beauty of Janet's Foss waterfall and this walk must be one of most spectacular in the Dales.

Gordale Scar – a good place to look for raven in the early spring

(🥾) ❶ Turn left out of the car park and proceed through the village, bearing left at the junction following signs to Malham Tarn and Arncliffe. After climbing uphill for a short distance out of the village look for a path on the your right hand side signed to the cove. Follow the path and head to the RSPB watchpoint near the foot of the cove. Take the path leading left up the steps to the top of the cove.

ⓘ The peregrine is a truly remarkable bird, capable of reaching speeds of over 160 km (100 miles) per hour. The RSPB watchpoint at Malham Cove provides an excellent chance to see this enigmatic raptor in the spring and summer months. You may see the peregrines terrorising the local pigeons or the first tentative flight of the young (usually around late June/early July). The young chicks are always given names. One year they were named 'Clint' and 'Gryke' after the blocks and fissures of the limestone pavement above the cove.

There is more to the cove area than just peregrines, however, with the watchpoint ideally placed to observe breeding little owls. The little owl is our smallest owl species and was introduced into Britain in the nineteenth century. The species is at the northernmost edge of its

British range in the Dales but seems to have found the area much to its liking now the winters are less hard than they once were. Tawny owl may also be seen, and fenceposts should be scanned for spotted flycatchers and redstarts. Listen for the yaffling call of the green woodpecker, though for such a colourful bird it can prove amazingly difficult to see. House martins usually live up to their name and nest in eaves in houses but here they make their mud-based nests on the face of the cove. Grey wagtail and dipper may be seen on the stream if the path has not become too busy with tourists. Away from birds, the area is good for both stoat and weasel (much to the consternation of the nesting little owls) and you may be fortunate enough to see a fox. The limestone pavement on top of the cove is home to scarce plants such as harts tongue fern, wood-sorrel and enchanter's nightshade.

❷ **At the top of the cove bear right across the limestone pavement to a stile. Head over the stile following the path signed to Gordale. Follow this path, crossing the Malham Rakes road, to reach Gordale. Here you can turn left and then shortly after left again to head towards Gordale Scar. It is recommended not to attempt to scramble up to the top of the scar as this can be tricky. Retrace your steps back to the road and head back along it towards Malham before taking the path signed off to Malham on your left. Janet's Foss is soon to be seen on your left hand side. Near Malham bear right at the three-way signpost and then cross the stream by the stepping stones or footbridge further along to return to the car park.**

Gordale Scar was carved out by a meltwater channel beneath an overlaying ice-sheet and is now an imposing gorge. The cliffs support many breeding jackdaws and you should look for the largest member of the crow family, the raven. Wheatears are common in spring and summer and this is another area to look for green woodpecker. Approaching Janet's Foss, the senses are bombarded by the smell of wild garlic and possibly the sight of a resplendent male goosander. The waterfall itself is small but magical and provides a fantastic setting to watch redstarts and willow warblers in the surrounding trees. Sharp eyesight and some luck could even see you rewarded with a sighting of Jennet, the local queen of the fairies who lives behind the waterfall and lends her name to it! Return to the village to be greeted by the screams of the swifts that nest in the eaves of buildings and the possibility of refreshment in the cafés or pubs.

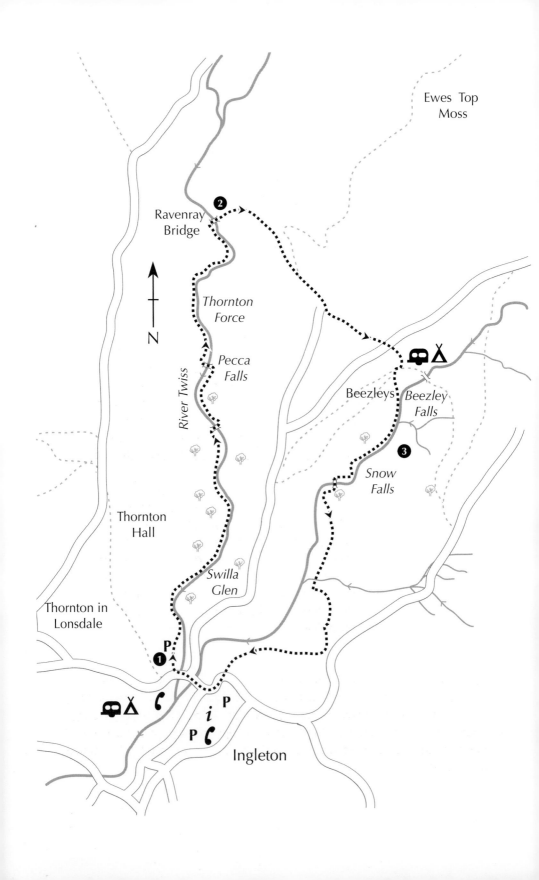

Ewes Top
Moss

Ravenray
Bridge

2

N

*Thornton
Force*

River Twiss

*Pecca
Falls*

Beezleys

*Beezley
Falls*

3

*Snow
Falls*

Thornton
Hall

*Swilla
Glen*

Thornton in
Lonsdale

P

1

P

i

P

Ingleton

Ingleton

The waterfalls walk

Thornton Force

Length: 7 km (4.5 miles)

Time: 3 to 4 hours

Season: Late April to late June is best

Terrain/grade: Easy/moderate in places

Start: Ingleton waterfalls walk car park, SD693734

Bus/train: The number 80 bus runs between Lancaster and Ingleton (Monday to Saturday). The 567 Stagecoach service runs between Ingleton and Kendal (Monday to Saturday). Kirkby Lonsdale coaches run a 581 service between Settle and Ingleton Monday to Saturday. All buses stop at the Tourist Information centre

General: A ticket needs to be purchased for the walk. The current charges are £4.50 for adults, £2 for under 16s and £9 for a family ticket. The trail is open seven days a week from 9 a.m. Note that the paths can become very crowded during the day on weekends or bank holidays. Refreshments and toilets are available at the start of the trail and there is a snack van near Thornton Force

THIS WALK IS ONE of the most impressive in the Yorkshire Dales. The quiet beauty of the woods makes an excellent contrast with the tumbling torrent of Thornton Force or the spectacular ravine of Baxenghyll Gorge. With a wealth of woodland birds and the opportunity for good views of our familiar river species the only difficulty lies in an overload of things to admire!

(人) ❶ **The entrance fee is payable by driving up to a kiosk past the café and toilets. Park the car beyond the kiosk and then head along the well-marked track veering left with picnic tables on your right. The trail is then straightforward and easy to follow as it winds up past Pecca Falls and Thornton Force.**

❶ The picnic tables alongside the River Twiss provide an excuse for an early pause and can be a good point to look for dippers on the river whilst the long-tailed tits and chaffinches flit through the trees. Moving up the trail you soon reach a series of steps as you begin to enter Swilla Glen. Look for spotted flycatchers preying on the insects gathered in the shade of the glen. In the next section between Swilla Glen and Manor Bridge, the woodland birdwatching can be excellent in the spring and early summer. Pied flycatchers compete for attention with the restive blackcaps and garden warblers. The birdwatcher is also given a rare chance to see five different species of tit in a small area. The familiar blue, great, coal and long-tailed tits are joined by the rarer marsh tit. The black cap and bib, plain brown plumage and loud 'pitchou' call help to distinguish this scarce bird from its commoner cousins.

Beyond Manor Bridge, your attention can switch from ornithology to geology as you cross the North Craven Fault. Despite its dramatic-sounding name you could easily not realise you were crossing such an important feature. A small tunnel in the bank on your left marks the fault and was the product of an unsuccessful search for lead. More easily visible are the Pecca Falls, which provide an impressive sight from the bridge across the river. The grey wagtails certainly seem to think so as they can often be seen downstream of the bridge. The woodland up towards Thornton Force might provide a view of the bounding flight and pied plumage of the great spotted woodpecker. The river below the waterfall holds the plump and quirky dipper. Thornton Force itself is the best-known feature of the entire walk as the River Twiss plunges 12 m (40 feet) down. After wet weather it is a particularly powerful sight, so ideally your visit would be in glorious sunshine after dismal weather in the previous week!

(人) ❷ **Cross Ravenray Bridge after Thornton Force and follow the path up the hillside, making sure you turn right along the lane heading towards Beezley Falls. The lane heads down, skirting Twistleton Farm, and you then need to cross a minor road before**

reaching Beezley Farm. Follow the track right signed Beezley Falls, then take the narrow gravel track on your left.

❶ The footpath across the hillside to Beezley Farm provides a pleasant change with the limestone karst scenery of Kingsdale and imposing sight of Ingleborough ahead. The white rump of a wheatear is a familiar sight in this area as it moves between perches on scattered boulders. Crossing the minor road, look to your left for the stonechat on the drystone walls. Winter might produce a roving raven in this area whilst summer brings the chatter of swallows nesting in the barns.

❸ **The trail along the River Doe is easy to follow as it passes Baxenghyll and Yew Tree gorges. At the end of the trail follow the lane as it curves down the hill before taking a narrow right down Sammy Lane. Take the second left to pass by the open air swimming pool and follow the path as it takes you to the road. Turn right and cross the bridge to return to the waterfalls walk car park.**

❶ The walk back along the River Doe is an enchanting trail of waterfalls and gorges. Beezley Falls and the chasm of Baxenghyll Gorge are the highlights whilst the nuthatches and redstarts ensure the birds cannot be forgotten. Look for wood warblers, which still cling on here despite declining elsewhere in the area. After crossing a bridge the path begins to move away from the riverside, though before it does so check the river banks for grey wagtails. They take advantage of the relative quiet here to nest.

Moving up into the younger woodland it is difficult not to be struck by how numerous willow warblers are in the spring and summer months. Long-tailed tits are full of character and keep any walker entertained, whilst treecreepers climb quietly up tree trunks. Kestrels patrol the scars as you near the end of the walk. Descending into Ingleton gives the chance to see an open-air swimming pool apparently rated the fifty-second best in the world and built by unemployed miners in 1933. Take your swimwear and give it a go on a summer's day! A spotted flycatcher perched on the telephone wires along the road as you enter the car park could provide the perfect finale to a spectacular walk.

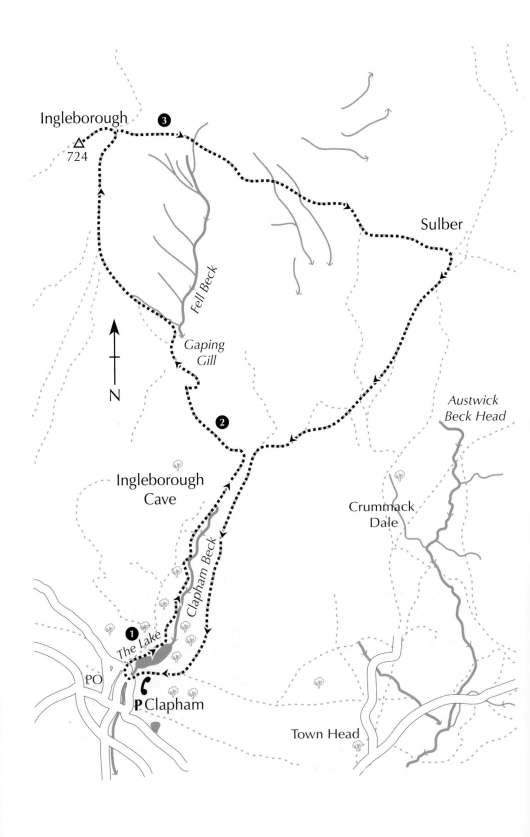

Clapham

A trip for dotterel up Ingleborough

Dotterel

Length: 19.5 km (12 miles)
Time: Allow 7 hours
Season: Late April to late May and late August/
September for dotterel, but first two weeks of
May are best
Terrain/grade: Challenging
Start: National Parks car park in Clapham
Bus/train: Trains run to Clapham on the Airedale line
from Leeds to Morecambe. Note that the
train station is 1.6 km (1 mile) south of the
village. Kirkby Lonsdale Coach Hire run the
581 service between Ingleton and Horton that
stops in Clapham (Monday to Saturday)
General: Toilet block by car park, refreshments Clapham

THIS IS A FAIRLY strenuous ascent of an ever popular Dales peak, but the
rewards are great for those willing to take on the challenge. Attempting
the walk in the few weeks from late April to mid May will give you the
chance to see the rare and beautiful dotterel. The sight of this enigmatic and
confiding wader on the summit is surely the best way to forget tired legs. The
walk also offers the opportunity of visiting Ingleborough show cave or taking
a slight detour to see the 95-metre-deep-pothole, Gaping Gill.

❶ **When leaving the car park turn right, towards the church and
proceed to cross the bridge. Turn right after the bridge and follow
the road round until you see a farm on the right hand side and
a sign for Ingleborough Cave. This marks the start of the Nature
Trail, for which there is a small charge. Follow the trail past the
lake and cave and turn left to Trow Gill.**

❶ The nature trail through the woods provides an excellent and colourful start to the walk in spring. The floor is likely to be carpeted with blue bell and primrose. Look out for the range of exotic rhododendrons which were collected by the botantist Reginald Farrar. Bird song is rich and varied, with locals such as the blackbird or the robin competing with the descending trills of the numerous willow warblers and the melodies of blackcaps and garden warblers. Keep an eye out for woodcock on a spring morning and be alert for pied flycatcher as you near the end of the nature trail. Winter is likely to be quiet but the tit flocks, comprising blue, great, coal and long-tailed, help to keep avian interest alive and they might periodically be panicked by a roving jay. The ever popular tree-climbing residents, treecreeper, nuthatch and great spotted woodpecker, are all present along the trail and should be seen at any time of year. As you begin to leave the woods behind check the beck for dipper and listen for the yaffle of the green woodpecker.

⚘ ❷ **Scramble up Trow Gill and continue over the stile to the obvious track leading up to Little Ingleborough. From here the path is well marked up to the summit of Ingleborough itself, though you will need to take a short detour right to see Gaping Gill. To reach the triangulation point you will need to head west for a short distance after reaching the summit plateau.**

❶ Trow Gill is perhaps best known for being the scene of a great Dales mystery. A skeleton was discovered there by two potholers in 1947 but the remains could not be identified. The presence of cyanide, which was used by enemy spies in the Second World War to commit suicide if their cover was blown, led to a suspicion that the skeleton probably belonged to a German spy.

Now the birdwatcher should check Trow Gill for the more pleasant discovery of a redstart or spotted flycatcher, both of which are present in good numbers here. The walk up from Trow Gill to Ingleborough is less likely to be filled with birds, though an occasional ring ouzel can be seen at Clapham Bottoms in spring. It is well worth the short detour to Gaping Gill to see Fell Beck descending dramatically into the dark chasm. Every Spring and August Bank Holiday the local pothole clubs winch members of the public down Gaping Gill into the floodlit Main Chamber. Time your visit on these days and you would have a chance of seeing dotterel and the possibility of an unforgettable experience in Britain's biggest cave chamber.

Dotterel, Ingleborough, May 2007 – 2 of a 'trip' of 11 birds

If you are aiming to see dotterel on Ingleborough summit, visit in late April, the last two weeks of May or even in late August/early September. But to maximise your chances a visit on a relatively calm day in early May is best. Check the summit of Little Ingleborough on your way up and then search the summit plateau of Ingleborough carefully. Dotterel can be very confiding but take care not to disturb these rare waders. Try approaching them by walking sideways and you should obtain good views. As you take a well-earned break on the summit look and listen for the raven as it searches the area for carrion. Those brave enough to attempt the walk in the autumn and winter months could be rewarded with the fantastic sight of a snow bunting, a scarce and hardy bird that can cope with the harsh winter conditions on Ingleborough plateau.

❸ **Retrace your steps from the triangulation point and then descend towards the southern slopes of Simon Fell. Bear right as you descend and follow the well-trodden path which passes a ruined shooting hut. You can turn off right shortly after this to take a shortcut but the path here is faint so it is best to enjoy the limestone pavement and head through it towards Sulber. Turn right at the sign marked BW Clapham and head south-west looking down into Crummack Dale. The path splits several times but always bear right to avoid being taken down into**

Crummack Dale. Once on Long Lane the path is straightforward and takes you to Thwaite Lane. Turn right, signed to Clapham, and descend through the tunnels to be brought back into the village by the church.

❶ The charming wheatear is a real feature of the next section of the walk as you pass through spectacular limestone scenery. They can often be seen on Ingleborough summit but become particularly numerous perched atop the scattered boulders and drystone walls around Sulber. There is a wealth of other wildlife on offer here with the impressive emperor moth possible on the heather areas of the Allotment (to the south of the path as you skirt Simon Fell). In the limestone pavement area around Sulber the scarce bird's eye primrose can be seen in the wetter areas whilst hart's tongue fern grows in the shaded grykes. If you come across rock rose look out for the northern brown argus butterfly which can give an almost silvery appearance as it flies restlessly. In spring the air rings to the cries of curlews and you might be lucky enough to see a peregrine before you drop down onto Long Lane. Clapham then beckons with the prospects of rest and refreshments to soothe the legs after a tiring but wonderfully fulfilling walk.

Wharfedale, Littondale and Nidderdale

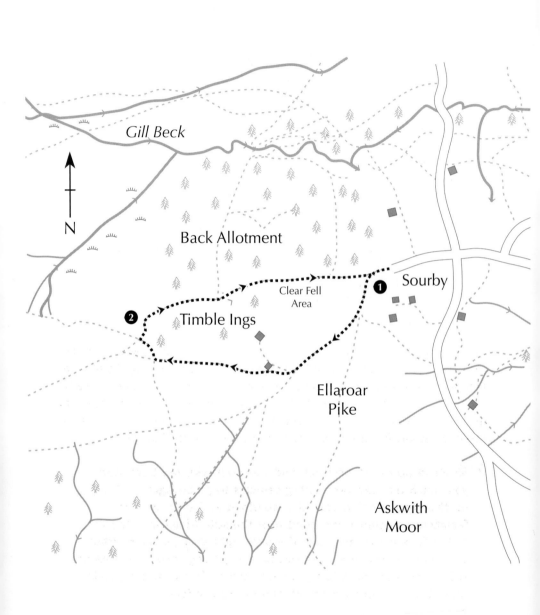

Gill Beck

N

Back Allotment

❷ Timble Ings

Clear Fell
Area

❶ Sourby

Ellaroar
Pike

Askwith
Moor

Timble Ings

In search of the 'gabble-ratchet'

Nightjar

Length: 3.5 km (2 miles)

Time: Allow 2 hours

Season: Mid May to mid July

Terrain/grade: Easy

Start: Limited parking for around 5 cars in the layby on your left about 200 m (220 yards) down the track past Sourby. The track is off the minor road between Blubberhouses and Otley, SE166530

Bus/train: None

General: No refreshments

THIS IS A FANTASTIC walk for the adventurous birdwatcher seeking out the nocturnal birds that can be hidden from view during the day. To see the nightjar, or 'gabble ratchet', you need to make this a late evening or very early morning walk (you are best advised not to go alone and to take a torch just in case). On a still night in the summer months midge repellent is also a useful accessory for this walk in search of a rare and fascinating bird.

❶ **Head up the stone track and bear left with the track when you reach the sign prohibiting vehicles to go straight on. Keep on this stone track across the moorland and then, with the farmhouse to your right, head over the stile (don't take the track to the farmhouse) and take the path right through the heather. Take care as this area can become very boggy after wet weather. Follow this path on a fairly straight course before turning right when the path splits near the end of the conifers.**

❶ Leaving the car, listen for chiffchaffs and blackcaps giving the dusk chorus. The first section of the walk skirting Timble Ings provides an opportunity to see the rare and mainly nocturnal long-eared owl. They hunt the fields alongside the track and around the farmhouse, particularly when they have young to feed from around mid May onwards. Be careful with identification as short-eared owls can also be seen here. Long-eared owls lack the white trailing edge to the wing of short-eareds and the wings appear more uniformly brown with a smaller and more orange primary patch near the wingtip. Their tails are more finely barred and a good view might reveal the piercing orange eyes and streaked belly. Curlew and lapwing feed in the fields whilst kestrel and sparrowhawk both regularly hunt the area. The moor is also the home to the red grouse, while a green hairstreak might be seen here to satisfy the butterfly enthusiast. The edge of the conifers could produce a rare sighting of the cuckoo. Redpolls, and the scarcer crossbills, move busily around the plantation and are best detected by their calls.

(🚶) ❷ **Follow this path round to a wooden gate on your right, after which you skirt the plantation and then head through it. Soon you reach a more open area where the path appears to split four ways. Carry straight on, with the fence to your left and you will reach a clear fell area on your right-hand side after around 200 m (220 yards). Continue along the track which takes you directly back to the car.**

❶ As you enter the conifer plantation, listen for the tawny owls that breed here. The streams and pools within Timble Ings are home to a good number of dragonflies and damselfies. Large red and common blue damselflies are fairly numerous and you might see the black body with golden rings of the scarce golden-ringed dragonfly. Roe deer, and occasionally red deer, are present and are best seen at dusk. Male woodcock perform their display, known as 'roding', over the tops of the conifers on spring evenings and utter grunts that add to the exciting atmosphere of nature watching at dusk. Pause when you reach a clear fell area on your right hand side a few hundred metres after the path splits. Look for tree pipits which display with their parachuting song flight onto the top of trees.

The main quarry to search for at the clear fell area, however, is the mysterious nightjar. Nightjars have been present here in the summer months in most recent years. Excellent habitat work at Timble Ings has facilitated the return of this bird to Nidderdale, where historically it was the stuff of legend and myth. In the late-nineteenth century locals called nightjars 'gabble ratchets', meaning corpse hounds, and many believed they represented the souls of unbaptised infants. Their reputation becomes understandable when you hear the mechanical 'churring' song of the male nightjar. This is an amazingly intense, prolonged and deep reeling sound that alternates between two gears and can only be heard when it really is late in the evening (usually after around 9:45 p.m. in June and July). When you hear the churring, scan the tops of the scattered bushes in the area for the elongated shape of the nightjar. When the churring stops look for the male flying with his white wing flashes and tail edges, which are usually just discernible in the failing light (use binoculars to see in rapidly diminishing light). With the 'squeaky gate' calls of young long-eared owls in the background, birdwatching can scarcely get any more spooky or exhilarating than this!

Long-eared Owl – Timble Ings is an excellent place to see this elusive species hunting

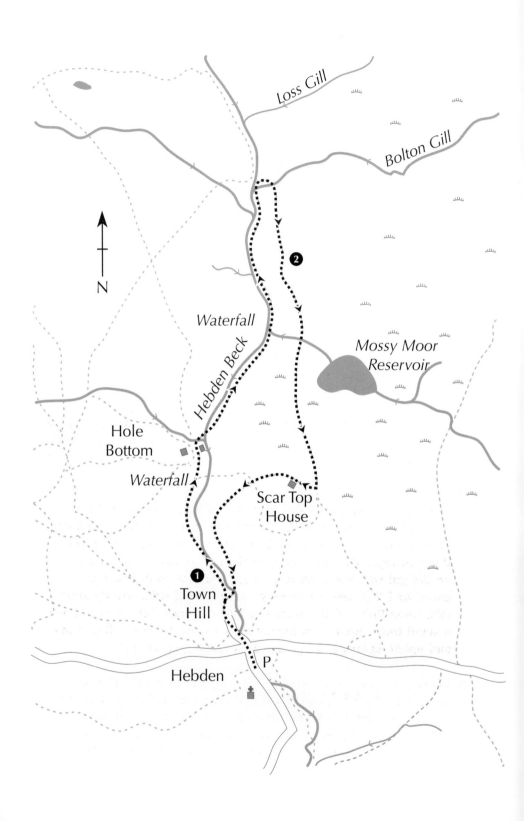

Loss Gill

Bolton Gill

❷

Waterfall

Mossy Moor
Reservoir

N

Hebden Beck

Hole
Bottom

Waterfall

Scar Top
House

❶

Town
Hill

P

Hebden

Hebden

Waders around Hebden

Lapwing

Length: 5.5 km (3.5 miles)
Time: Around 2 hours
Season: Late March to August
Terrain/grade: Moderate
Start: Parking possible in Hebden village, SE 026631
Bus/train: Pride of the Dales buses to Grassington and Skipton (Monday to Saturday)
General: Refreshments in Hebden village

THE WADERS THAT RETURN in the spring provide some of the most characteristic sights and sounds of the Dales. This walk is particularly good for the spectacle of the breeding waders and takes in the old mine workings above Hebden.

❶ Cross the main road and take the lane leading north. Keep on this lane, ignoring the first bridge to your right. Come to Hole Bottom and bear right through the wooden gate after Jerry and Ben's cottage. This track crosses the bridge and then leads you up the gill with the beck to your left. Pass through four more gates, and then see a ruin on your right-hand side. Shortly after this, when Bolton Gill emerges to join the beck, take a right along a small track. Bear right immediately on this track heading south and uphill, ignoring the grassy path leading up the gill.

❶ The lane leading up towards Hebden Gill provides a pleasant stroll and has plenty of birdlife to admire in the spring and summer months. Spotted flycatchers make dashes for insects from perches in the trees and are particularly reliable around Hole Bottom. Treecreepers cling to the trunks of trees lining the lane, whilst swifts scream overhead.

Crossing the bridge after passing Hole Bottom look for grey wagtail and dipper on the rocks. The walk up the gill is so tranquil, save for the shrill cries of oystercatchers and curlews that it is difficult to imagine that the area was once a hive of industrial activity. The spoil heaps remind the walker of the area's lead mining past. As you move further up the gill you can see the large chimney on Grassington Moor. Hebden Gill itself was crucial to the operation of the mines because the 'Duke's Level' driven into here drained the water that threatened to flood several hundred feet deep mine shafts.

Ring ouzels have clearly taken a liking to a landscape shaped by lead mining in the Dales (see Walk 26) and are often prominent up the gill in the spring. Check particularly the walls and tree to your left as you near Bolton Gill. The neat plumage of the male wheatear can be observed at close quarters here once they arrive in late March. His competitor in the beauty stakes comes in the form of the male stonechat, which is a recent colonist and tends to inhabit the areas of bracken. A little owl may perch obligingly on a wall if your visit is an early morning one. More to be expected is the tiny wren which belies its size by belting out a loud song from the bracken, whilst blackbirds see to it that the ouzels have competition from their more familiar cousin.

(𝕩) ❷ **Carry on this path as it takes you through a series of gates and skirts the hillside. When you come level with a house on your right hand side, turn right onto the track and over the cattle grid. Before reaching the gate to the house turn right along a grassy path that leads to a gap in the wall. Take the left-hand path downhill. Head through the wooden gate at the bottom and bear left in the field, continuing downhill. Follow the drystone wall as it veers left and you should see a stile ahead. Pass through another stile and then drop down to the beck and take the bridge across it. Turn left onto the lane and return to the village.**

❶ Moving along the hillside the waders that are such a feature of this walk become more evident. The lapwing is known locally as the 'tewit' after its frequently delivered call. Its buoyant flight and rounded wings give it a distinctive silhouette. If seen clearly in the fields before Mossy Moor reservoir you can appreciate the beautiful green and purple hue to the lapwing's plumage. Look for the white wingbars of a redshank in flight low over the fields whilst the curlew floats above. The reservoir provides a chance to see the long probing bill of the snipe as it feeds on the muddy edges. The black belly of the small dunlin is a scarce sight on the Dales moors, though Mossy Moor provides excellent habitat for it. The ringed plover might also be seen and passage periods in the spring and autumn have seen records of whimbrel, greenshank and little ringed plover.

Waders may try to steal the show but be alert for the other avian possibilities in the area. Red grouse are a regular sight and sound on the heather-clad areas and an evening or morning visit in spring or summer gives a chance of a short-eared owl near the reservoir. Lesser black-backed gulls stand imperiously on the reservoir edge, whilst teal are present here throughout the year. Winter brings occasional goldeneye and tufted duck to join the dabbling ducks and even the possibility of a hen harrier or peregrine causing panic amongst the wildfowl. Merlin hunt the area in the spring and summer months but are easily missed as they dash low over the surface seeking an unfortunate meadow pipit. As you continue past the reservoir, pause by the bracken on your right where the slowly delivered, simple tune of the reed bunting can be heard. Descending back to the beck and the village might allow you to finish the walk with the frequent glides and broad wings of a hunting sparrowhawk.

Snipe

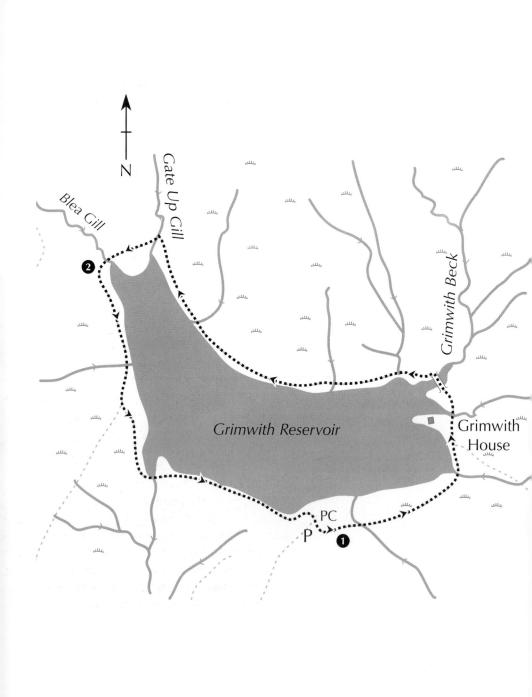

Blea Gill

Gate Up Gill

N

2

Grimwith Beck

Grimwith Reservoir

Grimwith
House

PC

P

1

Grimwith

Short-eared owls at Grimwith

Short-eared owl

Length: 7 km (4.5 miles)
Time: Allow 2.5 hours
Season: April to July best
Terrain/grade: Easy
Start: Large, free car park at end of approach road, SE 064640
Bus/train: A limited bus service runs between Harrogate and Grassington, Monday to Friday, and stops at the entrance to the lane leading to Grimwith
General: No refreshments. Toilet block by car park

THIS WALK AROUND GRIMWITH manages to combine wilderness and accessibility perfectly, with the windswept moorland easily negotiated thanks to facilities provided by Yorkshire Water. With the beguiling short-eared owl as the star bird of the walk there is every reason to relish a visit to the high moorland bridging Wharfedale and Nidderdale.

❶ **The walk is easiest to do anti-clockwise so head east on the track heading slightly uphill. When the path splits, either option can be taken as they meet again shortly. The track is easy to follow as it skirts the reservoir, though be sure to head over the bridge crossing Gate Up Gill in the north-west corner, ignoring the track leading uphill to your right.**

ⓘ Owls are a real enigma, being both ever popular yet seldom seen thanks to their nocturnal habits. This walk gives a chance to see the partly diurnal short-eared owl. The subtly varied, attractive plumage of this owl and its piercing yellow eyes make it a birdwatcher's favourite.

The population of the owl on Dales moors depends on the abundance of its main prey, the humble field vole, which periodically has population crashes and booms which cause fluctuation in owl numbers. Grimwith is an excellent place to see short-eared owls in any year, with a morning or evening visit in the spring or summer giving a chance to study the 'moor owl' as it is known in the Dales. Sightings are possible anywhere around the reservoir but be particularly alert in the north-east and north-west corners, on the mosses by Grimwith Beck and Blea Gill.

A great bonus of the Grimwith walk is that all the birds of the moorland can be seen, whilst ducks and waders on the reservoir add diversity to the species on show. Meadow pipits are abundant and are complemented by goldfinches on the thistles and willow warblers in the spring and summer in the developing plantations. Red-legged partridge are released here and their gaudy plumage can enliven a winter's day. The red wattle of the red grouse is a familiar sight and spring sees the grouse joined by wheatears and an occasional whinchat. The thatched barn you pass on your left at the south-east corner was rebuilt when the reservoir was constructed and dates back over three centuries. Oystercatchers perch on top admiring the cruck-built timber design. Scan the shoreline in the next section as it holds a few pairs of breeding ringed plovers. Check any plover you see for its dumpy shape and orange legs and bill base, as the sleeker little ringed plover has also been seen here recently. Buzzing redpolls may attract attention away from the reservoir edge as they move busily about the young trees.

🕭 ❷ **Be careful after crossing Blea Gill to take the track left keeping you close to the reservoir. This comes around 800 m (0.5 mile) after crossing Blea Gill, as the path turns slightly right and uphill. With a barn on your left and a Yorkshire Water sign facing away from you take the track left which returns you to the road. Head uphill and back to the car park.**

❶ The northern edge of the reservoir gives good views westwards towards Wharfedale and should provide a close encounter with the common sandpipers that favour the rocky shores. Raptors are always an exciting possibility at Grimwith, with hen harrier, buzzard and peregrine possible in the autumn and winter months and hunting merlins in the breeding season. As the path begins to bisect a bracken-covered slope look for the smart figure of the reed bunting. The north-west corner of the reservoir does not suffer from disturbance from yachting and windsurfing and can hold concentrations of wildfowl. Wigeon and teal are prominent in the winter months alongside the mallards and feral Canada geese and are occasionally joined by pochard, tufted duck and goosander. Lesser black-backed gulls powerfully patrol the area, whilst snipe and redshanks can sometimes be seen feeding at the muddy margins. Stock doves are present in good numbers in this corner and the young plantations can ring to the sound of willow warblers in spring. The reeling song of the elusive grasshopper warbler has been a feature in recent springs. The rushy area to your left as you begin the walk along the dam wall holds another member of the *Locustella* warbler family, the sedge warbler, in the summer months. The contented birdwatcher, having hopefully seen the moor owl, can return to the car park to the cry of oystercatchers along the dam wall.

Merlin

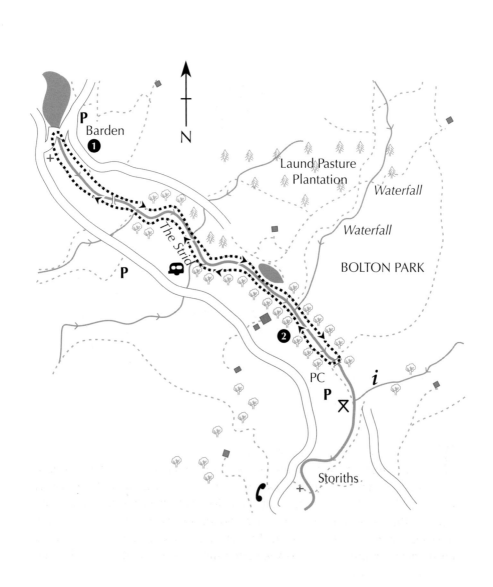

P
Barden ❶

N

Laund Pasture
Plantation

Waterfall

Waterfall

The Strid

P

P

BOLTON PARK

❷

PC

P

i

Storiths

Barden Bridge

Wood warblers at Strid Woods

Wood warbler

Length: 7 km (4.25 miles)

Time: Around 3 hours

Season: All year but best late April to June.
Note that the area can become very crowded
with tourists on summer weekends and bank
holidays.

Terrain/grade: Easy

Start: Free parking by Barden Bridge, though an early
arrival is needed here at weekends, SE053574

Bus/train: Pride of the Dales 74 service runs from Ilkley
and Grassington to Bolton Abbey (Monday to
Saturday). There is currently a limited service
run by Jackson's on Sundays in summer

General: Toilets and refreshments at the Cavendish
Pavilion and the Strid

THIS WALK HAS A strong claim to be one of the best birdwatching walks in
the Yorkshire Dales. If you are an aesthetic birder, moved by the colourful
and exotic looking, this is the walk for you. The typical stars of the Dales,
the kingfisher and the male redstarts and pied flycatchers, are complemented
here by the year-round presence of mandarin ducks. The popularity of the
area with tourists is testimony to the fact that this walk along the flat could
be an ideal compromise for the keen birdwatcher with a family or non-birding
friends to consider!

(🚶) ❶ **Take the path before the bridge signed to the Cavendish Pavilion. Follow this along the river and into the woods past the aqueduct. You will climb up through the woods and reach the road but stay on the path, descending the steps to a wooden gate. Follow the path across the bridge to the Cavendish Pavilion and then turn right signed Strid Nature Trails.**

❶ Starting at Barden Bridge means the walk could get off to an exciting start with a dazzling kingfisher. They often perch on the rocks or branches overhanging the river. Dipper, grey wagtail and goosander are all regular on the short stretch of river south of the bridge but the river merits special attention in the hope of locating the mandarins that have made the area their home. Although not a native species, the astonishing colour of the drakes and the subtle beauty of the females make them a welcome addition to the local avifauna. They can be seen in any month of the year, though in winter numbers can build up to over 40 birds. Look from Barden Bridge at the stretch of river north to Burnsall, and be alert for mandarin on the river around the Strid. As you move towards Strid Woods, you have the cry of oystercatchers and the aerial acrobatics of sand martins for company in the spring and summer.

Before entering Strid Woods, do pause to look at the impressive turreted bridge across the Wharfe. Although now very useful for the thousands of tourists seeking a circular walk around Strid Woods the main purpose of the bridge is as an aqueduct carrying water from the reservoirs in Upper Nidderdale (Walks 12 and 16). It is certainly to the liking of the dippers that regularly nest here. The rocks nearby can also be a good place to see the bobbing figure of the common sandpiper.

Moving on into the woodland you reach one of the best areas for birds. The nestboxes on the trees either side of the path here are regularly used by pied flycatchers. A patient wait at a respectful distance should give excellent views of this attractive species anytime from late April to around mid June. As the path climbs upwards redstarts can usually be seen and you should look for the wood warbler: this walk's star bird. If possible, listen to a recording of wood warbler's song before you go as it is distinctive and will greatly increase your chances of seeing one. The area before you reach Harrison's Ford shelter on your left is usually a reliable spot. The height you have gained here means that views can often be eye level and don't require the usual neck ache to see this superb but much declined bird.

🚶 ❷ **A clear track leads through the woods (the Green Trail) and can be followed to the Strid. Just past the Strid you can follow the signs to Barden Bridge or bear right to take a shortcut on a more rocky and uneven path which joins the main track. From here be sure to head right, signed to Barden Bridge, when the path forks and head underneath the aqueduct and back to the bridge. Cross the bridge to return to the car.**

ℹ️ Crossing the bridge by the Cavendish Pavilion check the river again for dipper, grey wagtail and goosander. Heading through the woodland towards the Strid, the air can be filled with the confusingly similar songs of blackcaps and garden warblers. Blackcap tend to have a shorter song which is more uncertain at the start and has a beautifully rich flourish at the end. The seasonal specialities are complemented here by the year-round presence of great spotted woodpecker, treecreeper and nuthatch. Lesser spotted woodpeckers are present but are highly elusive even in the early spring. As you approach the Strid look again for mandarin and search the beeches for brambling in winter. These attractive but very different species are similar in that they both fluctuate in number depending on the crop of beechmast in any given year. The area around the wildlife notice board near the Strid can be good for spotted flycatcher in the spring and summer.

Although the woods make a good bird-watching walk at any time of the year they are really at their best in spring, with beautiful carpets of bluebells and birds in full song in the trees above. If you can, try a visit for the dawn chorus in May to experience the woods at their most atmospheric and captivating. At times the birdwatcher has the welcome dilemma of choosing which fantastic bird to look at: even when out of the woods and heading back towards Barden Bridge there are orchids down below and green woodpeckers in the trees above, whilst an eye to the skies could reward with a red kite or even a spring osprey heading north to Scotland!

Red kite

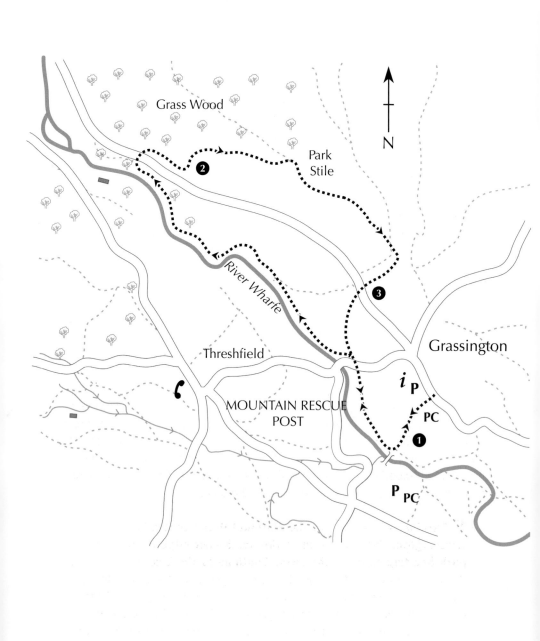

Grass Wood

Park
Stile

N

River Wharfe

Threshfield

Grassington

i P

PC

MOUNTAIN RESCUE
POST

P PC

❷

❸

❶

Grassington

The woodpeckers of Grass Woods

Lesser spotted woodpecker

Length: Around 8 km (5 miles)
Time: Allow 3 hours
Season: All year but late April to late June best
Terrain/grade: Easy
Start/finsh: National Parks centre, Grassington, SE002637
Bus/train: Pride of the Dales 72 service runs from Skipton
(Monday to Saturday). The 74 service runs
from Ilkley (Monday to Saturday). Limited
services run on Sundays from Keighley and, in
the summer, from Ilkley
General: Toilets at the National Parks centre.
Refreshments in Grassington village

THIS IS A GENTLE yet wonderful walk in terms of both scenery and wildlife. From the dippers diving into the pristine waters of the Wharfe by Linton Falls to the abundance of woodpeckers in Grass Woods, the walk is sure to have something for everyone. To see the carpet of bluebells in Grass Woods in spring or experience the vigour of the Wharfe at the Ghaistrills in winter is a great spur as you seek the birdlife of the area.

❶ **Parking is available at the National Parks centre in Grassington. Take the path at the south-east edge of the car park heading towards the river. Continue to the bridge, then take the right-hand path through the gate signed to Grass Woods. Continue on this path, crossing the road by Grassington Bridge. After crossing the road head down past the benches, through the wooden gate and down to the river. Follow the riverside path along to Lower Grass Woods.**

❶ The walk along the Wharfe provides an excellent chance to observe the special river birds of the Dales. The stretch of river from the wooden bridge to Linton Falls is usually reliable for the charismatic dipper and the restless grey wagtail. Watch out for an aquamarine flash as a kingfisher speeds by. In August and September these birds are particularly visible, as adults and juveniles alike disperse after breeding. In winter, expect an encounter with the compact little grebe or a solitary heron patiently stalking its next prey.

Spring sees the arrival of the noisy common sandpipers and oystercatchers. By early summer female goosanders parade their young on the Wharfe near Grass Woods. Look out for the agile sand martins as they hawk insects and return to their holes excavated in the river banks a few hundred metres either side of Grassington Bridge. Although the river is an obvious draw, the action is by no means confined to the Wharfe. From November, redwings and fieldfares arrive and the rowans and hawthorns prove irresistible to these attractive thrushes. If it has been a good year for beechmast (the nuts of the beech tree) brambling are likely, particularly around the Grassington Bridge area.

Dipper

Grassington Bridge – a good place to observe goosander and dipper all year round

❷ **Climb the hill into Lower Grass Woods and then bear right at the next two forks in the path, keeping a small wire fence to your right. Cross the road and head over the stile. Turn right onto the path nearest the wall. Follow this path to a beech plantation at the southern edge of the wood near the road. Head through the beeches and then bear left to pick up the path skirting the wall along the edge of the wood. Ignore any left turnings and head to Park Stile.**

Moving into Lower Grass Woods the smell and sight of many different wild flowers and the gentle flicker of a ringlet butterfly present a serene front that hides a somewhat murky past. The tale of the Grassington murderer Tom Lee is still told in the village to this day. It was in Grass Woods that blacksmith Lee robbed and murdered the local doctor,

Richard Petty, in 1766. Petty and Lee had both been to Kettlewell for the cockfights where the doctor had had a successful night. This sealed the doctor's fate and he never made it further back than Grass Woods. Lee was found guilty of the crime and hung on a gibbet at the entrance to the woods for all to see.

Comparable drama can now fortunately only be found in the natural world! The woods offer the chance to connect with all three British woodpeckers. Look for the green woodpecker around the Ghaistrills and Lower Grass Wood area, with great spotted likely throughout the woods. The lesser spotted is present here all year but is notoriously elusive. The best bet is to wait patiently by the Wharfe where the path begins to climb up the hill and look for the undulating flight of this tiny woodpecker as it crosses to the trees on the opposite side.

April marks the start of the period when the woods come alive with incoming summer migrants. The descending cadence of the willow warblers mixes with the melodies of blackcaps and garden warblers. The dawn chorus in early May can be breathtaking. Keen birders will strain their ears for the melancholy song of the redstart or the wonderful shimmering trill of the declining wood warbler. Look for the wood warbler when you take the path right just after entering Grass Wood. Spotted flycatchers and tree pipits often give good views in the more open areas of Lower Grass Woods. Check the trees on your right-hand side as you reach the top of the hill in Lower Grass Woods for the pied flycatcher. The approach to Park Stile is another good area for this distinctive species and the delightful plumage of a male redstart could be an added bonus here. These scarce summer visitors are complemented by residents such as the enigmatic treecreeper or the colourful nuthatch. If you can take your eyes off the birds of Grass Wood, look out for speckled wood butterflies. In May you might catch a glimpse of the rare speckled yellow moth which flies during the day.

❸ **Take the path heading to the right of the barn ahead. Follow the path through the field and keep right of another barn and head between two drystone walls. Head up the fields towards Town Head Farm, join the Dales Way footpath and then turn right onto Bank Lane. Head downhill on the lane past the benches. Cross the road at the junction and head straight on down the track. Pass through the metal gate and follow this path back to Grassington Bridge where you can retrace your steps back to the car park.**

❶ Leaving Grass Woods certainly does not mean the end of the birdlife of the walk. The barn at the end of the first field you cross is a good area for the little owl. This charming owl appears to be doing well in the Dales in the absence of harsh winters. Oystercatchers are an obvious presence in the fields in summer, whilst in winter fieldfares and redwings form large flocks in the area. The cave visible on your left is reportedly where Tom Lee went to hide from the authorities as they closed in on him. As you look back at Grass Woods, be alert for raptors as peregrine, buzzard, kestrel and sparrowhawk are all regularly seen over the woods. Following the lane, back towards the Wharfe look for tawny owls if it is nearing dusk or early in the morning. They often afford unusually good views here by perching on telegraph posts and chimneys. Following the river back gives a second chance to see the striking plumage of a male goosander or get a glimpse of a kingfisher to round off a walk in a fine Dales setting.

Little Owl: this species is regularly seen from the path skirting the edge of Grass Wood

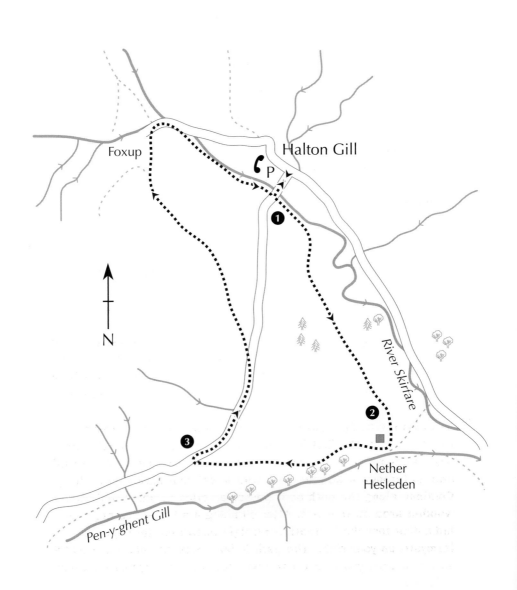

Foxup

Halton Gill

P

1

N

3

2

River Skirfare

Nether
Hesleden

Pen-y-ghent Gill

Halton Gill

The three wagtails walk

Yellow wagtail

Length: Around 8 km (5 miles)
Time: Allow 2.5 hours
Season: Early May to mid July
Terrain/grade: Moderate
Start: Parking alongside Halton Gill green with honesty box, SD881766
Bus/train: None available
General: Nearest refreshments at the Queens' Arms in Litton

THIS IS A REAL gem of a walk. It takes in two of the quietest and most attractive valleys in the Dales, Littondale and Silverdale. A visit in the spring or summer will give you the opportunity to see all three species of wagtail breeding in Britain whilst enjoying some truly impressive scenery.

❶ Cross the bridge and take a left signposted to Litton and Arncliffe. After the first field, the faintly marked path begins to move away from the river so keep right towards the drystone wall and go through a wooden gate with a National Park sign on it. Continue along the path as it passes a series of barns and then a wooded area on your left. After climbing a stile, notice the sign indicating that the footpath is straight ahead not through the farmyard on your right. The path is faint here but aim for a metal gate and once you reach it you will see a yellow-topped post and stile ahead.

❶ The walk really does start with a birdwatching bang as you take the path along the river. Although the yellow wagtail has disappeared from huge swaths of the Yorkshire Dales it still clings on here as traditional farming practices are maintained (meaning the hay is cut late enough in the year for the wagtails to breed successfully). Check the drystone wall bordering the first hay meadow on your right for this bright species. The male is vividly yellow and provides a fantastic sight amongst the more subtle colours of the Littondale landscape. Pied wagtails breed in close proximity and occasionally chase their scarce neighbour. Look for stonechat perched on the fences bordering the fields on your left. Action is by no means confined to the meadows as common sandpipers flick over the river. *Hirundines* can be a feature of the walk as swifts mix with the smaller swallows, house martins and sand martins to hawk insects over the water and meadows. Moving away from the river gives a chance to scan the valley sides for hunting buzzard and kestrel. You might just be lucky enough to spot a hen harrier riding the ridge in the winter months.

Stonechat

⚲ ❷ **After the stile head right, across the field, crossing a track to reach another gravel track. Go through the wooden field gate after the signpost for the Silverdale Road. Follow the lane through the houses bearing right up the hill and coming to a metal gate. After the gate take the grassy path up the hill, ignoring the tracks to your right and left. Keep on this path as it skirts a fence all the way to the road.**

❶ The middle section of the walk from Nether Hesleden to Foxup is most remarkable for its fantastic scenery. The walker can look down into Littondale and up Silverdale to Pen-y-ghent, Fountains Fell and Plover Hill. You will be kept company by the wheatears on the rocky hillsides and the noisy oystercatchers as you descend to Foxup. Kestrels hover over the slopes waiting to pounce on an unfortunate vole. Look carefully for the purposeful flight and diamond-shaped tail of the raven.

[*Walk continued after colour reference section*]

Mike Malpass

Mandarin

Few species can match the astonishing appearance of the mandarin. This exotic duck has recently colonised the Dales and added a splash of colour to the stretch of the River Wharfe from Burnsall to Bolton Abbey. Despite being a non-native species introduced into Britain from Asia, the mandarins seem at home and take advantage of the plentiful tree holes in the nearby woodland for nesting.

The male mandarin is a superbly colourful and unmistakeable sight. The more subtle olive and grey tones of the female are less striking but have their own beauty. Mandarins are present year round, though numbers can be at their greatest in winter, particularly if there has been a good crop of beech mast.

Walks: **9**, 15

Wigeon

Wigeons can be seen in the Dales throughout the year, though they are most easily seen in the winter months. Several hundred wigeon can be seen in the winter at favoured sites such as Hellifield Flash (Walk 1), Gouthwaite (Walk 16), or Semer Water (Walk 24). The small breeding population is confined to the moorland tarns or reservoirs such as Grimwith (Walk 8).

Mike Malpass

The male wigeon is an attractive duck, with his neat grey body contrasting with the reddish-brown head and cream strip on the crown. The female is much less distinct, with her rufous plumage having subtle variations that can only really be appreciated with a good view.

Walks: 1, 2, 7, 8, 16, 24

Mike Malpass

Teal

Teal are a dainty and attractive duck. They winter in good numbers on the reservoirs, tarns and lakes, with a few staying on to breed. Look for the chestnut head and grey body bordered by a horizontal white stripe of the male teal. The female is essentially brown, though in flight you should see a flash of green in the wing. Teal, like wigeon, are 'dabbling ducks', so-called because they prefer to upend to feed rather than diving underwater.

Walks: 1, 2, 7, 8, 16, 24

Mike Malpass

Little Grebe

This compact grebe is resident in the Dales. It breeds on the tarns and reservoirs in the summer months and can be found on the rivers in the winter. The winter plumage of the little grebe is essentially dull brown, but in summer it develops a deep purple plumage and makes a wonderful sight.

Walks: 1, 2, 9, 10, 15, 16, 21, 24

Mike Malpass

Goldeneye

Goldeneye are a real birdwatcher's favourite. The subtle beauty of the female and the splendid plumage of the male make the goldeneye the most appealing wintering duck in the Dales. Look for goldeneyes from October to March at favoured sites such as Malham Tarn (Walk 2) and Gouthwaite (Walk 16).

Walks: 1, **2**, 8, **16**, 24

Stan Craig

Tufted Duck

The tufted duck is a smart duck which can be seen in the Dales throughout the year, though numbers are greatest in winter. The male has an essentially black and white plumage, with the drooping crest that gives the duck its name. The female usually has a much smaller crest and is essentially brown in plumage. Tufted ducks, like goldeneye but unlike teal or wigeon, are diving ducks which feed by entirely submerging themselves beneath the water.

Walks: 1, 2, 7, 8, 16, 24

Mike Malpass

Goosander

The Goosander is a tree nesting duck which has made the rivers of the Dales its home. It is a member of the duck family known as 'sawbills' – so-called because of their numerous razor sharp teeth designed for catching fish. Goosanders can often be seen feeding vigorously, diving into the cold waters of a Dales river for considerable lengths of time and surfacing some way away from where the observer might be expecting. Other times you might see one loafing idly on a river bank enjoying a quiet knap.

The male goosander essentially looks black and white at a distance but a close views show a beautiful greenish gloss to the head and upperparts and a silvery grey tail. The female is basically grey with a reddish brown head

Walks: 2–5, 9–11, 13, 15–18, 21, 23–25, 27, 28, 30

Mike Malpass

Mike Malpass

Black Grouse

The enigmatic black grouse is at the southernmost edge of its range in England in the Yorkshire Dales. The male is an astonishing and unmistakeable figure with his blue glossed black plumage and lyre shaped tail. There is plenty of scope for gender stereotypes here as the males do not form pair bonds but instead display in a macho ritual known as the lek. Tails are fanned, weaker cocks attacked, and an evocative cooing noise is used to impress the watching female 'greyhens'. The most hearty display normally gets the girl but once they have mated the chubby blackcock leaves the female to incubate and care for the young on her own whilst he retires to moult!

Birdwatching holiday companies offer spring tours to Scandanavia and Eastern Europe with a chance to see the elusive black grouse early in the morning in clearings in the dense forests. Swedish or Polish birders would be shocked to visit Arkengarthdale and find black grouse strutting around in fields in the middle of the day with barely a tree in sight! They are indeed normally closely associated with forest but reduced grazing in East Arkengarthdale has seen a marked increase in the numbers of this much declined bird. If you wish to see black grouse try a visit in the period March to May when the highest numbers can usually be seen and avoid the summer when they moult and are elusive. Please be particularly careful if you come across lekking birds. Leks are a fantastic spectacle but if you are set on an early morning visit for this display be sure to abide by the Black Grouse Code of Conduct printed out in full in the front of this book. This will ensure this rare and wonderful Dales bird can continue to thrive and be enjoyed.

Walks: 20, **28**, 29, 30

Red Grouse

The 'Moorcock', as it is known locally, is the king of the Dales' moors. It is a hardy bird living in an inhospitable environment that is carefully managed for it by the shooting fraternity. Red grouse can be seen all year round on the heather moors of the Dales, though it may be best to avoid seeking them in the shooting season (particularly on the 'Glorious' Twelfth of August). Listen for its croaky 'go back' 'go back' call and look for the red eyebrows of the male grouse.

Given how heavily hunted it is, the red grouse can be very confiding. Birds can be seen perching boldly on gravel tracks allowing excellent views of their intricate and perfectly adapted plumage. Very occasionally a precocious male grouse, known as a 'rogue', will establish a territory and defend it vigorously. Anything that enters is attacked, including people or even cars!

Walks: 5–**8**, 11, 12, **14**, 15, 17–20, **25**, 26–30

Sparrowhawk (*opposite*)

The sparrowhawk is a widespread yet elusive raptor. It is relatively small in size, with a long and broad tail. The flight pattern is characteristic, with quick wingbeats interspersed with glides ('flap, flap, glide'). Sparrowhawks are present year round, with a healthy breeding population in wooded areas across the Dales.

All walks

Red Kite

No bird has been a more welcome addition to the dales avifauna that the red kite. A release programme started at Harewood House, near Leeds, saw reintroduced birds released into the wild. They soon spread to colonise the south-eastern Dales around Bolton Abbey and Barden. The kites are a spectacular and unmistakable sight and will hopefully spread further into other areas of the Dales.

Walks: 9, 14, 15

Stan Craig

Merlin

The merlin is probably the least often observed speciality of the Dales. Partly this is down to the inaccessibility of the bleak and lonely moors that are the merlin's home, but the bird itself can also prove difficult for the birdwatcher through its habit of flying low and fast over the ground. Look for the merlin's chief prey, the meadow pipit, taking to the skies in panic to alert you to the presence of this agile raptor. The merlin is so fast and nimble that it is able to catch moths as prey. The large and diurnal Emperor moth is regularly on the menu.

Merlins return to the Dales in March to breed and leave during late July and August. They generally disperse to winter on the nearest coastlines, though ringing studies have recorded Dales' merlins wintering as far a field as northern Spain.

Walks: 7, 8, **12**, 14, 15, 18–20, 25, 26, 28, 30

Mike Malpass

Kestrel

The characteristic hover of the kestrel as it searches for voles in the long grass is a sight that is familiar to most. This hunting technique relies on astonishingly sharp eyesight, enabling the kestrel to pinpoint the movement of voles and pounce on them with remarkable accuracy. Kestrels breed in tress and abandoned barns across the Dales and can be seen at any time of the year.

All walks

Stan Craig

Buzzard

Buzzards have made a phenomenal comeback to the Dales after suffering years of persecution. By the 1950s they were restricted to a few pairs clinging on in the north-west Dales but they are now widely distributed and are present throughout the year. Look for the characteristic soaring of the buzzard on 'V' shaped wings. A closer look will reveal a finely patterned plumage and a pale chest band. Check any buzzard in winter carefully, as rare rough-legged buzzards from Scandanavia occasionally visit the Dales at this time of year.

All walks

Peregrine

This fast and powerful falcon is doing increasingly well in the Dales, though sadly it still suffers from illegal persecution on some grouse moors. The short tail and sturdy build with broad based wings tapering to a point help to distinguish the peregrine from kestrel, merlin or hobby that all might be seen in the Dales. Malham Cove provides an ideal nest site, with plenty of ledges available for the peregrines to make a scrape high up on cliff face. Prey for the peregrines at Malham consists mostly of pigeons and rabbits. Pigeons seem to be an easy and favoured prey item, which goes some way to explaining why peregrines have taken so readily to nesting in the country's city centres. The peregrines seem to coexist happily with the jackdaws nesting on the cove but every now and then they fall out spectacularly – with the jackdaws always coming off worst!

Walks: 2, **3**, 4, 5, 10, 17, 18, 25, 28, 29

Mike Malpass

Hen Harrier

This magnificent raptor is sure to be a highlight of any birdwatching walk. Sadly it is much rarer in the Dales than it should be due to illegal persecution. Hen Harriers prefer to breed on the heather moorland, which brings them into direct conflict with the shooting fraternity who view the harrier as a threat to grouse populations. Attempts by the harrier to breed in a particular area of Nidderdale are consistently thwarted. The argument between conservationists and those with shooting interests on the grouse moors continues unabated and with no apparent sign of a compromise being reached.

The result is that the Hen Harrier is a rare sight in the Dales – a sighting is possible on any of the walks listed below but you would need a good deal of luck. For the brave, a walk over the moors in winter or early spring provides the best chance of seeing this elegant raptor. The female harrier is more regularly seen, with a sighting of the ghostly grey male a real treat.

Walks: 2, 7, 8, 11, 12, 14, 15, 16, 18, 19, 25, 26, 28, 30

Oystercatcher (*opposite*)

The oystercatcher is an instantly recognisable and characterful wader. The orange bill, pied plumage and loud 'keeep' call make oystercatchers difficult birds to overlook. Normally a coastal species, Oystercatchers spread into the Dales in the 1940s and are now firmly established. They return to the riversides as early as February and depart in the autumn.

Walks: 1, 2, 4, 5, 7–18, 20–30

Stan Craig

Dotterel

The dotterel is a beautiful and elegant wader that passes through the Dales in small numbers on its way to and from breeding grounds in the Scottish Highlands. Unusually, the female is brighter coloured than the male, and the male does all the incubation and the caring of the young. The bright colours of the dotterel did historically prove their undoing with scores of hunters seeking them out in the late nineteenth century high on the Wensleydale and Ribblesdale moors. The bright feathers were used as anglers lures and the tameness of the dotterel meant they stood little chance against the gunmen.

Now the dotterel are thankfully only sought by keen and energetic birdwatchers. High up on Ingleborough summit dotterels feed vigorously in spring as they near the end of their long journey from Africa. If you are patient, dotterels can be wonderfully confiding birds, but take care not to disturb them. Try taking your camera and sitting down at a respectful distance to let the birds get accustomed to your presence and approach closer. A calm day in the first two weeks of May is the prime time to see dotterel but even then a bit of luck is still needed to encounter a 'trip' of these delightful birds.

Walk: 5

David Mower

Stan Craig

Lapwing

Few sounds are more evocative of the Dales than the 'tewit' of the lapwing. It is a hoarse and drawn out call which fills the meadows and pastures of the Dales in the spring and summer months. A close view of a lapwing, with the purple and green glosses to its plumage, is a real treat. In flight the lapwing is equally distinctive, with its broad rounded wings and buoyant butterfly like flight.

All walks

Golden Plover

This graceful wader returns to its Dales breeding grounds as early as March and stays until the late summer. Listen for the high pitched whistle of the plover on the moors and high ground. Despite their superb plumage – with delicately patterned golden upperparts contrasting with the black underparts – the plovers can be hard to locate on the ground. Look in areas of burnt heather or raised bare patches in the rushy pastures.

Walks: 7, 8, 12, 19, 25, 26, 28, **30**

Mike Malpass

Stan Craig

Ringed Plover

The Yorkshire Dales holds a nationally important breeding population of ringed plovers. The rocky margins of Grimwith and Gouthwaite reservoirs are the favoured haunt of this compact and well-camouflaged wader. Its sandy plumage means the ringed plover can be difficult to locate on the shoreline and the observer needs to look carefully to pick out the orange bill and legs and black face mask.

Walks: 1, 7, **8**, 14, 16, 24

Little Ringed Plover

The little-ringed plover is a welcome recent addition to the breeding birds of the Dales. Previously unknown here, it is now a regular feature at sites such as Hellifield Flash (Walk 1) and Gouthwaite (Walk 16). To distinguish the little-ringed from the ringed plover, look for the slimmer build, more elongated shape and longer yellowish legs. A close view will reveal the yellow eyering, and dark bill. Little-ringed plovers are present from the early spring until autumn.

Walks: **1**, 8, 16

Mike Malpass

Mike Malpass

Redshank

The redshank is a scarce wader which breeds in the pastures and meadows of the Dales. The redshank's name gives away its most prominent identification feature: the red legs, though the leg colour is a little variable and juvenile birds in particular have legs which are more orange in colour than red. Listen for the loud, repeated piping call which often betrays the presence of a redshank.

Walks: 1, 2, 7, 8, 12, 16, 20, 24, 25, 28, 29, 30

Mike Malpass

Mike Malpass

Curlew

The return of the curlew to the Dales truly heralds the first sign of spring. From late February onwards its bubbling 'cour-lee' call echoes across the meadows and pastures of the Dales. Few birds are as recognisable by sight as the curlew. Its large size and long, decurved bill give this wader a distinct profile.

All walks

Snipe (*opposite*)

Snipe are a cryptic and secretive bird of the moorland and damp pastures. They are often first seen in flight as they shoot up unexpectedly from your feet, uttering a sharp 'catch' call and zigzagging speedily away. In spring listen for the 'drumming' display of the male snipe. Remarkably, the pulsating sound in this performance is produced by the air rushing through the tail feathers of the snipe as it descends from on high.

Snipe are present in the Dales year round, though most leave their breeding grounds in the winter. As they disperse, sites like Hellifield Flash (Walk 1) can hold up to a hundred birds in the autumn. They feed vigorously on the shoreline and afford unusually good views. Ringing studies have recorded snipe that bred in Nidderdale wintering in south-west Ireland and France.

Walks: **1**, 2, 7, 8, 12, 14, 16, 19, **20**, 24–26, 28–30

Mike Malpass

Common Sandpiper

'Common sands', as birders often refer to them, are a loud and vibrant wader that can be found on the rivers and streams of the Dales from April until September. The repeated trilling call is often the first clue to the presence of a common sandpiper. They are restless birds, with distinctive clipped, quivering wingbeats in flight and a constantly 'bobbing' body when perched.

Walks: 1–5, 7–18, 20–28, 30

Dunlin

The dunlin is a scarce breeding wader inhabiting the bleak moorland tarns of the Dales. Passage dunlin stop off at sites such as Hellifield Flash (Walk 1) and Gouthwaite (Walk 16) in the spring and autumn, but conservationists focus their studies on the small breeding population. Dunlins are small waders with long decurved bills. In summer, the black belly is the most distinctive plumage feature.

Walks: 1, 2, **7**, 8, 16, 24

Stan Craig

Great Spotted Woodpecker

Woodpeckers are one of the most popular birds, and rightly so. Their colourful plumage and unique 'drumming' on the trunks of trees has made them a favourite subject for cartoons and probably our most widely recognised bird family.

The great-spotted woodpecker is resident in the woodlands of the Dales. Listen for the sharp 'kick' call and look for the bounding flight of this woodpecker.

Mike Malpass

Those wishing to locate the much rarer lesser-spotted woodpecker should be alert for a significantly smaller woodpecker, with a shorter bill and white barring across the back.

Walks: 2–5, 7, 9, 10, 11, 13, 15, 16, 18–30

Cuckoo

The first cuckoo heard remains the barometer used by many to determine when spring has arrived. A fierce competition takes place in the letters pages of newspapers across the country to determine who has heard the first cuckoo. Anyone fortunate enough to hear a cuckoo in the Dales before the last week of April will stand a good chance of winning the local competition. Sadly hearing or seeing a cuckoo at all in the Dales can now prove difficult. This famously parasitic species has declined significantly but can thankfully still be enjoyed in small numbers in the spring and summer months.

Walks: 4, 5, 6, 9, 10, 12, 13, 14, 15, 16, 19, 22, 23, 25–29

Stan Craig

Mike Malpass

Short-eared Owl

There can be few better sights in the Dales than a short-eared owl quartering the moor on a fine spring morning. Known in the Dales as the moor owl, the local population of this bird depends on whether it is a 'good vole year' in which the chief prey item, the short-tailed field vole, is readily available. Amazingly considering the chief prey it is dependent on, short-eared owls do suffer from illegal persecution on a backward minority of grouse moors. Those wanting to see this captivating owl would be well advised to time their walk early in the morning or in the evening, though the early afternoon can also be a surprisingly good time.

Walk numbers: 6, 7, **8**, 12, 14, 15, 18, 19, 20, 25, 26, 28, 29, 30

Long-eared Owl

The long-eared owl is one of the Dales' rarest breeding birds. Its nocturnal and extremely secretive nature also makes the 'Leo' the most difficult species to find. A dusk or dawn trip to mature conifer plantations on the moor edge is required to stand a chance of a sighting. The best way to locate their presence is when there are young present (from around mid May onwards). The adults then have to hunt more frequently to feed the young; and the young themselves give their presence away with their characteristic 'squeaky gate' calls.

Mike Malpass

Long-eared owls can be tricky to separate in flight from short-eared owls. Look for the plainer wings and more restricted orange coloured patch on the primaries (outer wing). A better view might confirm the lack of a white trailing edge to the wings; the less boldly marked tail; and even the deep orange eyes.

Walks: **6**, 19, 20, 22

Stan Craig

Little Owl

The little owl is the smallest British owl species and is unusual in being partly diurnal. A sighting of one perched on a favoured wall or rock is possible at any time of day, though as ever your best chance comes at dawn or dusk. Little owls were introduced into Britain in the nineteenth century and are now a firmly established part of our avifauna. They are doing increasingly well in the Dales and are resident throughout the year.

Walks: 2, 3, 4, 7, 8, 9, 10, 13–16, 18, 20, 22–30

Stan Craig

Tawny Owl

The tawny owl is one of the most elusive species in the Dales. Despite being fairly widespread, the strictly nocturnal lifestyle of this owl makes seeing one a real challenge. Try an early morning walk in the spring, when young may be being fed, to maximise your chances of a sighting. Hearing a tawny owl is much easier: listen out for the classic 'hoot' of the male, and the loud rasping 'ke-wick' of the female.

Walks: 1–7, 9, 10, 11, 13, 15, 16, 18, 19, 21–30

Mike Malpass

Kingfisher

The kingfisher must be the most colourful and striking of all Dales birds. The brilliant aquamarine of the kingfisher is unmistakable and can brighten a winter's walk considerably. The flash of blue is often all you see as a kingfisher flies low over the river at speed. They are present in the Dales all year round and come spring excavate their nesting holes in the banks along the river (and pray the river doesn't flood!). The late summer can be an excellent time to see this superb species as family parties disperse and are often highly visible.

Walks: 2, 4, 5, 9, 10, 13, 15, 16, 18, 21, 23–25, 27, 28, 30

Skylark

The skylark is one of our most treasured birds. This humble lark has been much celebrated, with figures as diverse as Vaughan Williams and Bobby Sands taking inspiration from its song. The song is indeed the most memorable aspect of the skylark: a continuous and mesmeric sound delivered while the lark is suspended in the air. This sound can still be enjoyed in the Dales, with skylarks still relatively common, particularly in the grassy moor-edge pastures.

Stan Craig

Walks: 1–8, 11–20, 22–30

Stan Craig

Yellow Wagtail

The yellow wagtail is a vivid and unmistakable summer visitor to the hay meadows of the Dales. Its colour and habit of perching on drystone walls make it a prominent and much appreciated sight in the more remote Dales where it still clings on. Changes in farming practice, particularly the earlier cutting of the hay in late June and July when the wagtails are still breeding, have seen the yellow wagtail population decline markedly. Thankfully quiet Littondale and Malhamdale remain strongholds for this fabulous species. The wagtails arrive in early May and can still be seen alongside the rivers and streams of the Dales as late as early August.

Walk numbers: 1, 2, 11

Grey Wagtail

Grey wagtails add a splash of colour to the fast-flowing streams and rivers of the Dales. A few winter here but most only return in the spring to breed. The male is a particularly attractive bird, with his yellow underparts contrasting with the black bib and throat. The female is paler and lacks the black on the throat. Watch out for juvenile grey wagtails – with their lack of colour and short tails, they can confuse the inexperienced birdwatcher.

Walks: 3–5, 7–13, 15–18, 20, 21, 23–30

Mike Malpass

Mike Malpass

Tree Pipit

The tree pipit is known as a 'birder's bird', meaning most non-birders would never even realise its existence. A small and subtle brown pipit, it is very similar in plumage to its much commoner cousin, the meadow pipit. Not that this should put anyone off looking, for the rewards are great in taking on the identification challenge and locating this scarce bird. The tree pipit returns to the Dales in late April/early May and can be seen through until late July.

Listen for the distinctive song of the tree pipit and particularly the repeated whistle at the end. In spring, you can see tree pipits perform their parachuting display flight down on the tops of trees and bushes. Be aware that meadow pipits, whilst generally confined to the meadows, also perch in bushes and trees. If the pipit you see isn't singing, look for the larger size, thicker bill, and neater, more clearly defined plumage of the tree pipit. The streaking on the flanks (side) of the tree pipit is minimal and more restricted than on the meadow pipit.

Walks: 6, 10, **13**, 18

Meadow Pipit

The meadow pipit is the commonest breeding bird in the Dales. 'Mipits', as they are often referred to by birdwatchers, are present throughout the year, and indeed are one of the few species brave enough to stay on the high windswept moors during the winter. They are a rather featureless bird, with only their repeated 'seep 'seep' calls likely to draw the attention of the observer. For raptors, though, they represent a crucial prey item, with merlins in particular having a diet dominated by meadow pipits.

All walks

Mike Malpass

Steve Gantlett/Birding World

Ring Ouzel

The 'mountain blackbird', as it is fondly known, is both one of our most appealing and elusive breeding birds. A male ouzel perched proudly on a wall with his gleaming white chest is a sight even the most casual birdwatcher cannot miss. Yet although they are present in the Dales from around late March until as late as October, for much of this time they can seem almost invisible. Undoubtedly the best month to see ring ouzels is April when they establish territory from scattered trees and drystone walls.

Walks: 2, 7, 12, 25, **26**, 27, 30

Dipper

The dipper is an iconic bird of the Dales. It graces the most picturesque spots alongside the rivers Wharfe, Ure or Swale, where it can be seen plunging boldly into the water 'swimming' for insect larvae. It is a restless and characterful bird, with a stout figure, brown and white plumage and scratchy song. Dippers are present all year round on the rivers and streams of the Dales. Look particularly near bridges, as crevices in the stonework are a favoured nesting site.

Walks: 3–5, 7–11, 13–18, 20–**21**, 23–30

Mike Malpass

Whinchat

The fortunes of the whinchat and the stonechat in the Dales have reversed, with the whinchat now a decidedly tricky bird to locate. That there are only three walks in this book where whinchat is now a likely sighting says much for the scarcity of this species (though on almost any of the walks, a passage whinchat in spring or autumn is a possibility). In addition to the three walks mentioned, look for whinchat if you are ever passing through

Stan Craig

Coverdale or driving over the moors between Lofthouse and Masham as these areas remain good for this appealing chat. To distinguish whinchat from the commoner stonechat, look for the prominent white supercilium (stripe above the eye). Whinchats are present in the Dales from early May until August or even September.

Walks: 6, 8, **14**

Mike Malpass

Mike Malpass

Stonechat

The stonechat is doing increasingly well in the Dales thanks to a succession of mild winters. Bracken covered gills and rushy areas on the heather moors are the favoured areas for this species, though they do also occasionally nest in hay meadows. They are present throughout the year but often disperse in winter and leave the higher ground altogether during cold spells.

Walks: 4–8, 11, 12, **14**, 15, 17–20, **25**–30

Mike Malpass

Raven

The raven is a majestic bird which has made a welcome comeback in the Dales. Historically, ravens faced severe persecution in the Dales encouraged by the payment of bounties for their heads. The churchwardens account books for Dent show the princely sum of 5s. 10d. being paid for thirty-five raven heads in 1737. Ravens were mistakenly believed to be responsible for the loss of lambs, though in reality ravens feed

David Tipling Photography

predominantly on carrion and would probably be terrified by the sight of a healthy lamb.

The raven population was reduced to only a handful of pairs by the 1980s and '90s but is now slowly recovering despite continued persecution on some grouse moors. Ravens are present in the Dales year round, though numbers are supplemented in winter by wandering birds from elsewhere in the Pennines. In distinguishing ravens from crows, look for the larger size, thick neck and bill and diamond shaped tail. A variety of calls can be heard but the most common raven call is a rolling 'prruk prruk' croak.

Walks: 2–5, 7, 8, 11, 12, 14–20, 22, 25, 26, **27**, 28–30

Wheatear

Wheatears are the classic bird of the limestone scars and pavements of the Dales. In these areas, look for a bird flying off from a nearby rock or wall with a striking white rump and a 'chack chack' call.

Stan Craig

When seen perched, the wheatear is a very attractive species. The male is particularly striking, with blue-grey upperparts, a black mask and orange breast. Wheatears arrive in the Dales in late March and early April and can be present into September.

Walks: 2–8, 11–15, 17–20, 25–30

Redstart

The redstart is one of
the most attractive
and colourful species
breeding in the Dales.
It arrives in late April
and busily devours
insects in the woodlands
and hedgerows until
August when it begins
the long journey back
to wintering grounds in
Africa.

Most significant
areas of deciduous
woodland in the Dales
hold redstarts, but they
are often best seen in
scattered hillside
bushes or hedgerows.
Listen for the call – a
rising whistled
'huit' followed by
a quieter clicking.

Mike Malpass

The plumage of the
male redstart is stunning, with the orange breast, black face and white forehead making
a particularly fine sight. The female is duller and browner but shares the characteristic
quivering red tail.

Walks: 2–5, 7, 9, 10, **13**, 15, 16, **18**, 21, 23–30

Mike Malpass

Stan Craig

Wood Warbler

Wood warbler is a real birder's favourite, with its bright green and yellow plumage and unmistakable song. They have declined in the Dales though strongholds such as Strid Woods and Grass Woods in Wharfedale are still reliable places for this fantastic bird. Your chances of seeing one are greatly enhanced by learning its distinctive song. A wonderful shimmering trill, often likened to a spinning coin, it is a sound that makes a May morning in the woods a memorable one.

Walks: 4, **9**, 10, 15

Mike Malpass

Spotted Flycatcher

Spotted flycatchers have declined significantly at national level but are thankfully still a frequent summer sight in the villages and woodlands of the Dales. They arrive back from African wintering grounds in early May and can be seen through until early September.

Walks: 2–5, 7–13, 15, 16, 18–30

Mike Malpass

Pied Flycatcher

The pied flycatcher is one of the special birds that draws birdwatchers from far and wide to the tranquil woodlands of the Dales. 'Pied flys', as they are affectionately known, return to the Dales in late April to breed. Birdwatchers need to be quick off the mark to see this attractive species, as it becomes elusive after breeding and can be hard to locate after early June. The first two weeks of May are best.

Pied flycatchers seem to favour nestboxes, which explains why walks through Strid Woods and along the River Arkle are particularly good for seeing them. Listen for its simple whistling song and look for the smart black and white plumage of the male. The female is browner and less distinct but has a noticeable white patch in the wings.

Walks: 4, **9**, 10, 13, **15**, 16, 18, **23**, 28

Mike Malpass

Nuthatch

The nuthatch is a widely distributed Dales resident. In spring you might hear the distinctive song – a series of repeated 'guip' 'guip' notes or see the nutchatch plastering mud around the edge of its nesting hole to make it a more suitable size. In the winter, nuthatches often move from the woodlands to the gardens to take full advantage of the bird tables and feeders.

Mike Malpass

Walks: 2–5, 7, 9, 10, 11, 13, 15, 16, 18, 20–30

Treecreeper

The treecreeper is a wonderful bird: distinctive and quirky, yet unobtrusive and easy to miss. A normal sighting is of a bird running furtively up a tree trunk, hunting for insects in the bark and crevices. Closer study will reveal the long decurved bill and delicately variegated plumage. Treecreepers can be readily found throughout the year in the deciduous woodlands of the Dales.

Walks: 2–5, 7, 9, 10, 11, 13, 15, 16, 18, 20–30

Stan Craig

Mike Malpass

Reed Bunting

The reed bunting is a scarce and localised breeding species in the Dales. There are few areas of reed, which represents the classic habitat for this species, though birds in the Dales seem content to make do with rushy pastures or areas of bracken. Listen for the simple, slowly delivered song which can be transcribed as 'reed, reed, top of reed'.

Walks: 1, 2, 7, 8, 14, 16, 24, 29

Redpoll

This agile and restless finch is present in the Dales throughout the year, though it is most numerous and best seen in the spring and summer months. Redpolls have a distinct red patch

Mike Malpass

on the crown, a short yellow bill, and white underparts. Males have a striking bright red breast, making them one of our most colourful birds. Look for redpolls in the hawthorn and alder bushes, and listen for their reeling song flight.

Walks: 2, 4, 6, 8, 9, 10, 12, 13, 15, 16, **18,** 20–25, 27–30

Stan Craig

Siskin

The siskin is a delightful finch which can be seen throughout the year in the Dales. Large numbers are present in winter in some years, when birds from the continent migrate northwards and boost the numbers. Siskins are a real treat for those who feed the birds in their garden and often afford excellent views as they dangle on sunflower seed feeders. A small and increasing breeding population can be found in the coniferous woodlands.

Walks: 4, 5, 6, 7, 9, 10, 12, 13, 15, 16, 18–23, 25–30

Twite

The twite has sadly suffered a drastic decline in fortunes both in the Dales and nationally. A finch that used to be widespread on the moors is now confined to a few favoured areas such as Arkengarthdale and Silverdale (near Penyghent). The twite can be separated from its commoner cousin, the linnet, by the darker streaking on the underparts; the warmer tones to the plumage; and, in summer, the pink rump.

Walks: 11, 25, 26, 30

Stan Craig

❸ Turn right onto the quiet road. Head along it over a cattle grid and then look for a grassy path on your left as you near the brow of the hill. The path is easy to miss but is just opposite a layby on your right and you should be able to see the roadsign indicating a 17% gradient ahead (though if you reach this you have gone too far). This path leads you all the way to Foxup. Make sure you descend the hill when nearing the village and don't take the bridleway leading off to your left. Turn right onto the road and then take a right before the bridge onto the path signposted to Nether Hesleden and Litton. This leads you back to the bridge by Halton Gill.

❶ The last section of the walk along the river from Foxup to Halton Gill gives the chance of all three British wagtails in close succession. The grey wagtail is often present on rocks just downstream of the bridge and the more familiar pied gives itself away with its typical two-syllable call. Yellow wagtails breed in the hay meadows on your left as you near Halton Gill. They can be seen admiring their territory from a perch on top of a drystone wall and are the real stars of this walk in spring and summer. A sighting of the striking male completes a walk that gives a chance to admire one of our most characterful bird families in a hidden and beautiful part of the Dales.

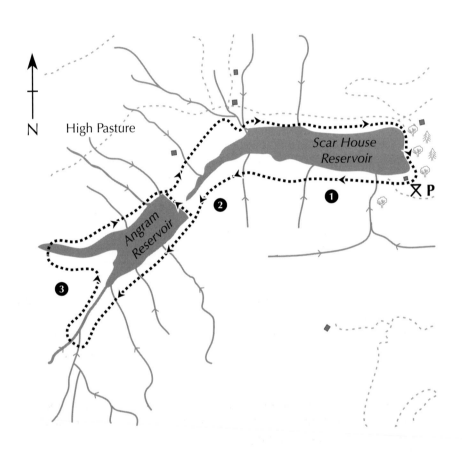

N

High Pasture

Scar House
Reservoir

Angram
Reservoir

❶

❷

❸

X P

Scar House

The merlin around Scar House and Angram

Merlin

Length: 6.5 km (4 miles) or 10.5 km (6.5 miles) for the longer walk
Time: About 2 hours around Scar House and 4 hours for the extended walk
Season: Late March to July
Terrain/grade: Easy
Start: Large and free Yorkshire Water car park at end of approach road, SE068765
Bus/train: The Nidderdale Rambler service runs on summer Sundays from Pateley to How Stean Gorge, 5 km (3 miles) away
General: No refreshments. Large toilet block by car park

THESE RESERVOIRS NESTLING IN Upper Nidderdale have a wild and desolate beauty, with the summits of Great Whernside and Little Whernside looming imposingly over them. Birdwatching here on a fine spring day with a merlin dashing over the lower slopes of Great Whernside can be a wonderfully fulfilling experience.

(🏃) ❶ **From the car park bear right alongside the toilet block and turn left onto the tarmack track. Follow this along the length of Scar House Reservoir to Angram Dam.**

❶ Birdwatching can start from the car park at Scar House, with wheatears and the shy ring ouzel on the limestone scars above. Spotted flycatchers sometimes pose on the wires as you head towards the reservoir, whilst redpolls buzz and the more familiar house martins feed vigorously overhead. The reservoirs themselves hold relatively few birds save for feral Canada and greylag geese, a few lesser black-backed gulls and cormorants. It is mostly the rocky foreshore and surrounding moors that command the attention of the birder. Look for common sandpipers, which can usually be found in the south-east corner. They typically bob their tails up and down when perched on a rock and have fast, clipped and quivering wingbeats in flight. This gives them what birdwatchers refer to as a distinctive 'jizz' (meaning an overall impression of a bird's identity based on structure and behaviour). Oystercatchers are another feature of the rocky shore and make a fine sight with their almost comical orange bill and pied plumage.

Scar House — the beginning of the walk around the reservoir

Scar House Dam – a good vantage point to look for
crossbills, siskins and redpolls

The rushy moorland edge to your left as you skirt Scar House Reservoir is home to good numbers of breeding waders. Lapwing, curlew, redshank and snipe should all be seen in spring. Merlin occasionally hunt here so listen for the reactions of the waders and pipits to alert you to the presence of one. They are a super sight with their purposeful flight and slender wings but they can prove surprisingly elusive for the birdwatcher. This is partly because they hunt low over the ground, meaning they can be easily missed unlike other birds of prey that clearly break the horizon. Merlins are less vulnerable than other raptors to illegal persecution because they prey overwhelmingly on meadow pipits and starlings, with red grouse chicks only very rarely taken. The winter months are best for other birds of prey, with the rare rough-legged buzzard possible at this time of year. Be vigilant even when driving along the approach road to the reservoir as they have been recorded here. This Scandinavian visitor can be distinguished from the common buzzard by the extensive white in its tail and paler and more contrasting underwing. Searching for raptors in winter always requires perseverance and a bit of luck. The potential reward of an elegant hen harrier or a rough-legged buzzard is more than enough incentive though!

(walker) ❷ **From here you can opt for a shorter walk heading across the dam and then turning right onto the grassy path leading along the side of Scar House Reservoir. When you meet a junction after crossing a stile turn right downhill then turn left at the bottom, signed for Scar House Dam. Cross the dam and turn left to return to the car park.**

ⓘ Wheatears are a welcome feature of the walk around Scar House in the spring and summer months. You should also see red grouse and the introduced red-legged partridge. Stoats allow only quick glimpses as they hunt stealthily along the pastures and foreshore. The black tip to the tail distinguishes them readily from the weasel and in winter you may be fortunate enough to spot one in its white ermine.

The walk finishes on an interesting note as you cross the impressive Scar House Dam. The reservoir was constructed between 1921 and 1937, with Angram Reservoir preceding it. The workers building the huge dam wall lived in the lively village of Scar House. It is difficult to imagine today that the village had a gym, a hospital, a canteen and even a cinema! Aside from the history, the dam wall provides a good vantage point for birdwatching. The winter months see occasional crossbills in the conifers. Spring sees the return of blackcaps and the charismatic cuckoo. Cuckoos are now a infrequent sight and sound in the Dales but the dam wall here gives a great chance to see one in the spring. Siskins breed in the plantation below. This most attractive finch can be seen here alongside redpolls and the more expected goldfinches, mistle thrushes and goldcrests.

(walker) ❸ **For the longer walk, do not cross the dam. Instead, take the path along the edge of Angram Reservoir. In the south-western corner of the reservoir cross the beck over a footbridge and then bear right to a metal gate. The ground beyond gets boggy and the path fainter as it follows the reservoir edge with scattered waymarker posts. Bear left, slightly away from the reservoir edge, to a crumbling drystone wall and then follow it before the path takes you left towards the north-west corner. Cross the bridge here and bear right at the top of the hill. Follow the path along**

Angram and then at the dam take the grassy path signed Scar House Circular. When you meet a junction after crossing a stile, turn right downhill then turn left at the bottom signed for Scar House Dam. Cross the dam and turn left to return to the car park.

For the energetic birdwatcher the extension to Angram is likely to reward the effort with rugged scenery and another chance to see the star bird of the walk, the merlin. Be vigilant in the south-west corner of the reservoir as this area is often hunted by merlins after their arrival in late March. As you cross the footbridge over the beck, check for grey wagtails and also for the stonechats which are usually present in the rushes and bracken. Over 130 years ago Joseph Lucas wrote his *Studies in Nidderdale*, in which he stated confidently that there were no stonechats in Nidderdale but that whinchats were extremely common. Now the stonechat has colonised the dale and appears to be increasing, though the whinchat has declined to a scarce and localised species. As you continue around the remote reservoir, with common sandpipers and a few grouse for company, look for a short-eared owl quartering the moor or a raven overhead. Return to Scar House and the chance of siskins and a cuckoo to finish the walk in style.

Short-eared owl

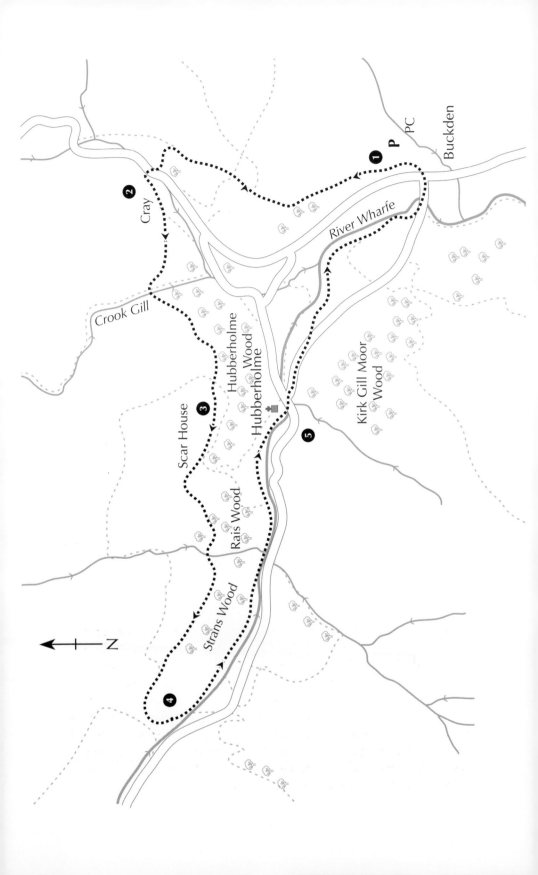

Buckden

Langstrothdale and the tree pipit

Tree pipit

Length: 11 km (7 miles)
Time: About 4 to 5 hours
Season: Best late April to July
Terrain/grade: Moderate
Start: Pay and display parking at Buckden YDNP car park, SD942773
Bus/train: Pride of the Dales buses from Ilkley, Skipton and Grassington stop in the National Park car park (Monday to Saturday). A limited service currently runs on summer Sundays from Ilkley
General: Toilets at the car park in Buckden. Refreshments at Buckden, Cray and Hubberholme

THIS IS A DELIGHTFUL circular walk combining superb scenery and excellent birdwatching. You will follow the River Wharfe as it heads up the beautiful Langstrothdale, with a wealth of birdlife including the sought-after tree pipit on the way.

❶ **Take the stony track leading up an incline from the car park signed Buckden Pike/Cray High Bridge. After ascending Buckden Rake when the track splits, leave the stony track to take the grassy left-hand path which runs alongside a drystone wall. Continue on this path until you are opposite the farm at Cray in the valley below. A faint and easily missed path runs left downhill to Cray by a drystone wall. Take this, keeping right by a wall and then through the gate at the bottom. Descend to Cray, crossing the beck to reach the White Lion. The beck is normally very easily crossed but take care after wet weather.**

Redstart

ⓘ The walk starts on a stony track known as Buckden Rake. The Rake used to be the old Roman Road leading north past Semer Water to the fort at Bainbridge. This section not only promises superb views once you climb out of the wood but also excellent birdwatching. The scarce tree pipit, always much sought after by birdwatchers, arrives in Rakes Wood from its African wintering grounds in late April. The open area on your right about 150 yards past the wooden gate is an excellent place to stop to search for this subtle pipit. Check the same area of scattered trees for the orange flash of the redstart's tail. The pied flycatcher is likely to prove more difficult to spot, though familiarity with its simple five-note song gives a greater chance of success.

As you climb out of Rakes Wood take a minute to savour the scenery. The view here is arguably the best in Wharfedale and on a clear day admiring the infant Wharfe in the valley below can be wonderful. The path along to Cray skirts the lower slopes of Buckden Pike and is the year-round domain of the kestrel. The wheatear returns here in late March or early April to herald the start of spring. Take care crossing the beck as you head to Cray as you may be distracted by a nearby grey wagtail. The White Lion at Cray can provide early refreshment for the birdwatcher, though most of the walk and plenty of birds lie ahead.

(🕏) **❷ Take the track to the right of the White Lion signed Stubbing Bridge and Yockenthwaite. Climb up past the farms, ignoring the left-hand path leading off, and pass through a wooden gate with the signpost reading Scar House and Yockenthwaite. Continue on this path, crossing a small stream and then following a fence to your left across the hillside.**

ⓘ As you climb past the farm above the White Lion look out for redstart and spotted flycatcher, which are both present in the spring and summer months. Swallows feed vigorously on insects here whilst charms of goldfinches flit delicately around the trees. The path now takes you along the flat, skirting the top end of Hubberholme Wood and allowing appreciation of the glaciated U-shaped valley of Wharfedale. Examine the hillside near Crook Gill for a variety of wild flowers, including harebell, pignut and kidney vetch. Listen for the yaffle of the green woodpecker, though they can prove difficult to see despite their size and colourful plumage.

(🕏) **❸ On reaching a house to your left, ignore the left path signed to Hubberholme and follow the path over a stile as it bears left, signed Yockenthwaite. The path is then fairly easy to follow, though be sure not to climb the hillside after Rais Wood and instead bear left slightly. Above Yockenthwaite Pass through a gate and then turn left onto a stony track descending to the hamlet.**

ⓘ Rais Wood is another recommended place to stop. Both pied and spotted flycatchers are on show here in May and early June. After you pass through Rais Wood be aware that the next section can provide good views of tree pipits. Singing tree pipits may be heard almost anywhere from Cray to Yockenthwaite but the limestone pavement area above Strans Wood gives a good opportunity to study the fine detail of their plumage. The thicker

Pied flycatcher

bill and limited streaking on the flanks are the classic features distinguishing tree pipit from the similar meadow pipit.

④ At Yockenthwaite bear left on the path signed Dalesway and Hubberholme. Follow the signs leading you to a narrow path along the river edge.

Descending to tiny Yockenthwaite brings new habitat and the prospect of an array of different wildlife in the former hunting grounds of Langstrothdale. The hay meadows in the valley are amazingly rich in flora, with herbs and grasses abounding and rarer species such as frog orchid and fragrant orchid present. Bird's eye primrose is common in the damper areas, and the gentle river is home to all the best-loved Dales water birds. Goosanders fly along the valley whilst dippers and grey wagtails pose obligingly on rocks and shingle banks. In spring the quietness of the area disappears when the common sandpipers and oystercatchers return. There are otters in the area but this is the most elusive mammal in the Dales and a sighting would require an early morning visit and a good deal of luck.

Buzzard

(🚶) ❺ **The footpath takes you all the way to Hubberholme, where you need to turn right after the church onto a stone track leading you to the road. Cross the bridge over the river and then turn left onto the lane. Follow the lane and after about 500 m (0.3 miles) you will see a barn on your left-hand side. The turning left is 150 m (165 yards) beyond this and signed to Buckden Bridge. This path takes you along the river and then out at Buckden Bridge. Turn left over the bridge and return to the village.**

❶ Buzzards are a regular sight on a sunny day, soaring on the thermals with characteristic V-shaped wings. As you enter Hubberholme look around the church for spotted flycatcher. If you have time, the small church, St Michael and All Angels, is well worth a look. It dates back to the twelfth century when it was a forest chapel within the great hunting forest of Langstrothdale Chase. It is most unusual for still having an original rood loft, one of only two in the county that survived the Elizabethan Reformation. The observant visitor will spot the small mice carved into the pews by the famous Thompson of Kilburn in 1934. Across the road the George Inn also has a rich history and still hosts the 'Hubberholme Parliament'. This has convened every year since the eighteenth century, though the tradition dates back even further, and sees local farmers gather in January to bid for grazing rights on sixteen acres of pasture owned by the church. J.B. Priestley used to enjoy a pint or two here and his ashes were buried in the churchyard. With fascinating history, scenery and birdlife, Langstrothdale really is a magnificient place. You could even spot a kingfisher from the riverside path back to Buckden to round off a walk that's difficult to better.

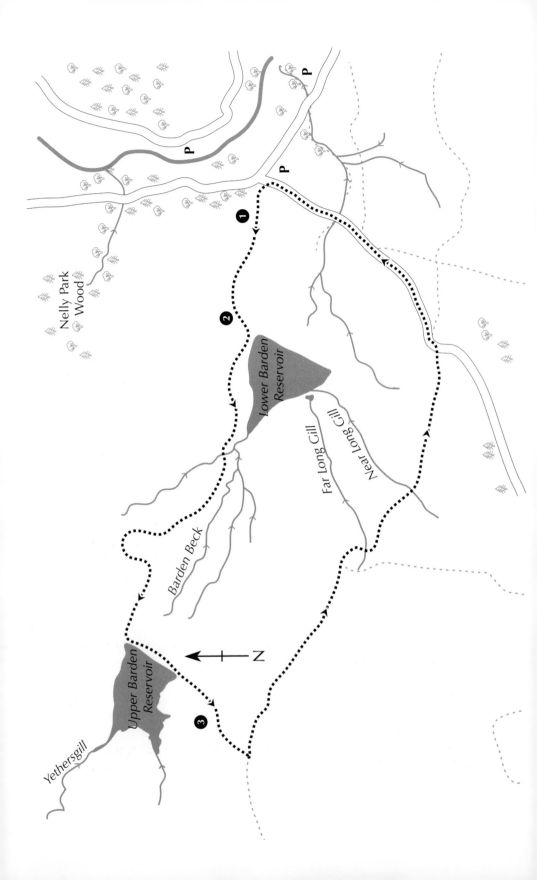

Nelly Park
Wood

P
P
P
P

1

2

Lower Barden
Reservoir

Far Long Gill

Near Long Gill

Barden Beck

N

Upper Barden
Reservoir

3

Yethersgill

Barden Scale

Two chats around Barden

Whinchat

Length: 12 km (7.5 miles)
Time: Allow 5 hours
Season: April to August
Terrain/grade: Moderate
Start: Limited parking at Barden Scale, SE051567
Bus/train: Pride of the Dales 74 service runs from Ilkley to Grassington and will stop at Barden (Monday to Saturday).
General: There is the small Priests House restaurant adjacent to Barden Tower. Otherwise the nearest refreshments, along with toilets, are at the Strid.

B ARDEN PROBABLY ATTRACTS MORE birdwatchers than anywhere else in the Yorkshire Dales, and with good reason. With the colour and majesty of the soaring red kite and the noise and activity of the black-headed gull colony, this is a birdwatching walk different to any other in the Dales. Only the wildlife can break the tranquillity of a summer's day walking through these heather-clad moors.

❶ Cross the road from the car park and go through the gate to take the track leading to Lower Barden reservoir.

❶ It is worth spending some time before the walk at Barden Scale looking across the valley to Barden Fell. A dedicated group of birdwatchers is often positioned here looking for birds of prey. Patience and persistence have been rewarded with up to eight different raptor species in one day! Red kites should be visible throughout the year if the weather is good, often soaring on the thermals with buzzards. Look for the forked tail and drooping wings of the kite as opposed to the buzzard soaring on typical V-shaped wings. Kestrels and sparrowhawks can often be seen from the viewpoint. During the spring and autumn migration periods, you might be lucky enough to see an osprey, goshawk or marsh harrier. Consistent coverage by birdwatchers here has helped to highlight the changing status of particular birds in the Dales. The hobby is becoming an increasingly regular sight in the summer months and seeing a raven is now a real possibility.

(🧍) **❷ Keep on the gravel track, ignoring the left turn down to the start of the lower reservoir. Continue to Barden Lodge, where the path veers left downhill and you can then bear right uphill to walk alongside the edge of Upper Barden Reservoir.**

ⓘ The next section of the walk up towards Upper Barden reservoir gives the birdwatcher the chance to see two species of chat in quick succession. Look for whinchat when a grassy track leads off to your left as you approach Lower Barden. Whinchats have a prominent supercilium (stripe above the eye) which easily separates them from the stonechat. Stonechats can be seen around Lower Barden and in the bracken areas between the two reservoirs. Look particularly in the bracken near the stream on the approach to Upper Barden (when the path takes a big curved detour). This area is also good for the attractive reed bunting, whilst linnets are present in good numbers between the reservoirs. Lapwing, curlew and snipe represent the waders, whilst the handsome red grouse can be seen very well from

Red grouse

the track. Cuckoos are often heard around Lower Barden and sometimes seen perched on wires. The rocky gill linking the two reservoirs provides habitat for the shy ring ouzel, which is best sought in April before the breeding cycle has begun.

Lower Barden reservoir itself is often relatively birdless, though the resident Canada geese and mallards should be visible. Occasionally it will reveal a surprise, such as a party of whooper swans stopping off briefly on their way north in spring or a common scoter in late summer. The edges of the reservoir should be checked for ringed plover and common sandpiper. Once at Upper Barden reservoir, it is time to experience the raucousness of the several-thousand-strong black-headed gull colony. The colony is a hive of activity in the spring and summer months. Great entertainment can be had watching the birds attack any invader, from lesser black-backed gulls to Canada geese!

❸ At the end of the dam follow the obvious stone track heading uphill with a line of grouse butts to your right (though you can take a shortcut leading left along a more faint path through the heather). Follow this track as it weaves uphill for nearly a kilometre (about three-quarters of a mile) before turning left as you near the brow of the hill. Follow the track as it takes you back to Halton Heights where you need to turn left over the cattle grid and follow the road back to the car. Be careful on the road, particularly on weekends when it can be quite busy.

Be alert for birds of prey on the walk back from Upper Barden reservoir. Peregrine and merlin can both be seen dashing over Barden moor in the spring and summer. The larger buzzards and red kites drift more languidly overhead. Short-eared owls should be looked out for, particularly on an evening or early morning excursion. Winter months can be bleak here but an occasional hen harrier or raven might reward the brave.

Barden Moor can be a productive place for many different forms of wildlife, with butterflies present including green hairstreak and small copper. Stoats and weasels are frequently seen and in winter you might be able to see a stoat in its white ermine. In April and May the male emperor moth flashes orange as he flies around the moor during the day. With the possibility of little owl from the road on the way back there is plenty of entertainment to help the walker forget about tired legs. Those with the energy can visit nearby Barden Tower, built in the fifteenth century by the shepherd Lord Henry Clifford, to round off a fine birdwatching walk with some absorbing history.

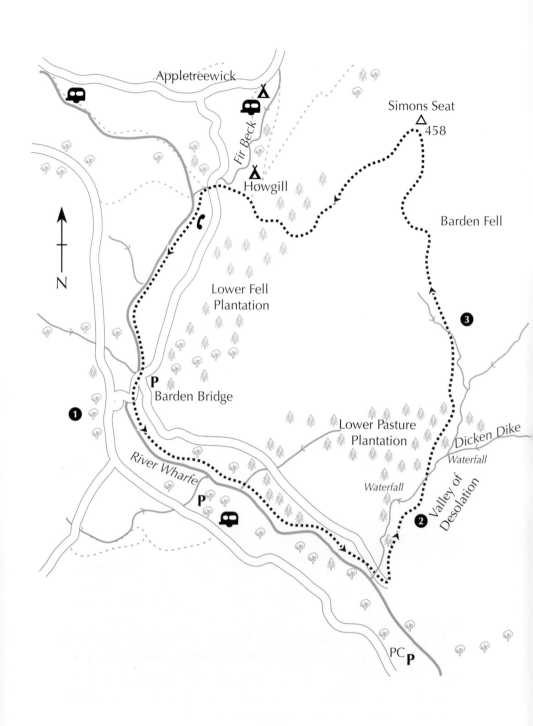

Appletreewick

Fir Beck

Howgill

Simons Seat
△
458

Barden Fell

Lower Fell
Plantation

3

N

1

P
Barden Bridge

Lower Pasture
Plantation

Dicken Dike

Waterfall

River Wharfe

Waterfall

P

2 Valley of
Desolation

PC **P**

Barden Bridge

Flying kites up Simon's Seat

Red kite

Length: 13 km (8 miles)
Time: 6 to 7 hours
Season: All year (best late April to June)
Terrain/grade: Moderate/challenging
Start: Free parking by Barden Bridge, though an early arrival is needed here at weekends, SE053574
Bus/train: Pride of the Dales 74 service runs from Ilkley and Grassington to Bolton Abbey (Monday to Saturday). There is currently a limited service run by Jackson's on Sundays in summer
General: Refreshments and toilets available nearby at the Strid and the Cavendish Pavilion

Y OU SHOULD SEE MORE BIRDS on this walk than any other featured in the guide. In May the birdwatcher might be overwhelmed by the array of different species on show. There is excellent woodland birdwatching at the start and a wealth of raptors throughout. With a chance to see moorland specialities around the fine viewpoint of Simon's Seat there is variety and excitement from start to finish.

❶ From Barden Bridge, take the path heading south along the river signed Cavendish Pavilion. After passing the aqueduct on your right, the path climbs up through the woods and takes you out by the minor road leading to Storiths. Leave the path and turn right uphill on the road. You will shortly see Waterfall Cottage on your left and here you need to take the path to your left signed Valley of Desolation.

❶ The start of the walk offers suberb birdwatching along the River Wharfe. The stars of the river, the kingfishers, dippers and grey wagtails, can all be seen along the stretch from Barden Bridge to the aqueduct. After the aqueduct, your attention should turn to the exciting possibilities of the woodland. The abundance of warblers in spring and summer include the scarce wood warbler. Pied flycatchers use the nestboxes on either side of the path and live alongside the more familiar nuthatches and treecreepers.

❷ Follow this path up the valley, passing the waterfalls to your left and then crossing a small footbridge over the Posforth Gill. Continue up the valley, bearing left uphill towards the conifer plantation as signed. Head through the wooden gate and follow the path through the plantation onto the open moor.

❶ As you move into the Valley of Desolation it is time to look for the target bird of the walk, the red kite. Scan North Nab ahead and watch the reaction of crows in the open area to your right. Kites can be seen from the Barden Scale raptor viewpoint (Walk 14) but they are usually distant, whereas this walk can provide great views of this stunning bird. They are present all year round in the area but are most easily seen on a sunny day. The kites colonised the area after being released at Harewood House near Leeds but this knowledge does little to diminish the appeal when one flies majestically overhead.

The Valley of Desolation, with its series of attractive waterfalls, provides a wonderful setting to see the red kites. The name of the valley was derived from the scene of devastation after lightning and rain in 1836 produced a storm surge from Posforth Gill which flattened all the trees in the area. It is a good place to see a range of common birds, from the smart bullfinch near Posforth Force to the goldcrests and treecreepers present in the plantation above. Birds of prey are a feature, with sparrowhawk, kestrel and buzzard all regular. Sightings of raven are increasing and North Nab can be a good place to see them, particularly in the winter months. In the spring check the valley sides and hillsides for wheatears and the more difficult ring ouzel.

❸ Once through the woodland follow the well-cairned stone track to Simon's Seat. Retrace your steps for a short distance after stopping at the trig point before picking up the obvious path heading south-west to Howgill. Continue on this path, which takes you downhill and through the conifers to Howgill. Cross Howgill

Lane and head straight on the narrow path between the houses. This takes you out to a lane, with a bridge over Fir Beck to your right. Cross the lane and join the path signed to Barden Bridge. Continue on the Dales Way back to Barden Bridge.

ⓘ The track now climbs steadily towards Simon's Seat but the birdwatcher should still remain alert for raptors. The thrilling sight of a hen harrier hunting the moor is possible in the winter months, whilst spring heralds the return of the merlins. Merlins are likely to be seen dashing low across the moor, though you may see one perched on a boulder or even displaying high up in the early spring. Short-eared owls breed on the moors and an early morning or evening visit gives the chance of seeing one fly buoyantly over the heather. The characteristic moorland birds – the meadow pipit, wheatear and red grouse – should all be seen from the path towards Simon's Seat. Simon's Seat itself provides a fine view across Wharfedale and in the winter months the birdwatcher has a chance of seeing snow buntings there. Look out for tawny and little owls as you descend towards Howgill, particularly in the evening. As you near the end of the walk, be aware that the stretch of river between Howgill and Barden Bridge can be good for the astonishingly exotic-looking mandarin.

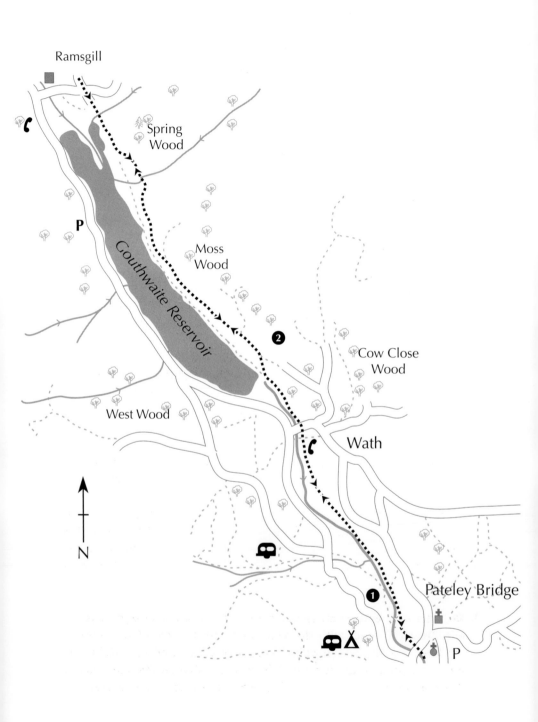

Ramsgill

Spring
Wood

P

Gouthwaite Reservoir

Moss
Wood

2

Cow Close
Wood

West Wood

Wath

N

1

Pateley Bridge

P

Pateley Bridge

Winter raptor spectacular at Gouthwaite

Hen harrier

Length: Around 15 km (9 miles)

Time: Allow 5 to 6 hours

Season: All year (birds of prey best November to March)

Terrain/grade: Easy

Start: Pay and display parking in Pateley Bridge, SE158655. Parking in Southlands is limited to 4 hours, Nidd Walk is a longer stay car park

Bus/train: The 24 bus service runs all week between Harrogate and Pateley Bridge

General: Toilets and refreshments Pateley Bridge. There is the Yorke Arms in Ramsgill but check you are happy with the prices beforehand!

GOUTHWAITE RESERVOIR IS A magnet for birdwatchers visiting the Yorkshire Dales and justifiably so as it offers a different and enticing selection of species. Its fame lies mainly in its status as a winter raptor watchpoint, from which the moors above the reservoir can be scanned for birds of prey without having to endure the cold and effort of walking on the higher ground. This walk starts in Pateley Bridge and so gives a chance to see birds of the river and woodland before you reach the ducks, waders and raptors of Gouthwaite itself.

❶ In Pateley Bridge cross the main road with the bridge to your left. Over the road, with the Mill Lane sign in front of you, take the lane bearing left downhill. Follow this lane and turn right onto a narrow path where indicated by a small sign on the wall. Follow this narrow enclosed path as it skirts the edges of the houses

and brings you out by the river. Follow the path for about 1.6 km (1 mile) as it begins to move away from the river along a raised embankment. On this raised section, with a fence to your right, look for a visible path leading off left through a gap in the wall and take this to lead you to the road by Wath Bridge. Cross the road and continue on this path as it takes you to the dam at the southern edge of Gouthwaite Reservoir.

❶ The first section of the walk involves a pleasant stroll along the River Nidd and a taste of the birds Nidderdale has to offer. Where the river can be seen through the trees check for dippers and grey wagtails. You might see the flash of blue as a kingfisher hurtles past low and fast. Check the trees lining the route for a selection of commoner species, from residents like treecreepers and long-tailed tits to summer visitors like chiffchaffs and blackcaps. Winter sees the arrival of fieldfares and redwings from Scandinavia, and these attractive thrushes can often be seen stripping the rowans of their berries. Fieldfares are usually the more numerous but look for white supercilium (stripe above the eye) and reddish flanks of the redwing.

🚶 ❷ **Once at the dam, bear right uphill to a gate. After the gate turn left onto a stone track and continue on this as it descends towards the reservoir edge. Bear left when the path splits and ignore the track leading right uphill to High Holme Farm. Follow the Nidderdale Way up to Coville House Farm and beyond to a Yorkshire Water viewing area with a bench on your left-hand side. It's probably best to stop here and then retrace your steps back to Pateley Bridge. It is possible to make the walk a circular one by heading to Ramsgill and then following the Nidderdale Way along the road and using the viewing platforms along the western edge of the reservoir. This route isn't really to be recommended, however, as the road is narrow and can be very busy, particularly at weekends.**

❶ Pause at the dam wall as this is a good area for woodland birds. Spotted flycatchers make their forays for flies from the fences, while great spotted woodpeckers climb the tree trunks. Green woodpeckers are comparatively common in the woodland all along the east side of Gouthwaite. This colourful but shy bird can be surprisingly difficult to see, though here you have as good a chance as anywhere in the Dales. The trees lining the path along the reservoir can be good for redstart in the spring and summer and be sure to listen for the familiar sound

Gouthwaite reservoir: one of the most popular birdwatching sites in the Dales

of the cuckoo. The fields up the hillside, besides hosting a sizeable resident flock of Canada geese, can hold many lapwing in late summer and autumn.

Despite the birdlife elsewhere, the birdwatcher will inevitably be drawn to checking the reservoir itself. Although the whole of Gouthwaite is worth investigation, the best area for birds is the northern half of the reservoir. Tufted duck and teal breed, with goosander present throughout the year, but it is in winter that the numbers and variety of ducks are most notable. Tufted ducks increase in number and are joined by a few pochard. The superb white and black body and green-glossed head of the male goldeneye is a treat for the birdwatcher here, with numbers of this pretty duck building to as many as forty birds in winter. Occasional scarcities noted in the winter months include scaup and smew.

Spring brings falling water levels and the return of the waders to Gouthwaite. Common sandpipers breed on the rocky shore whilst lapwing and snipe tend to nest in the rushy areas at the northernmost edge. Both species of ringed plover nest, with the nationally rarer little ringed plover actually commoner than ringed plover here. Look for the more slender build and longer-legged appearance of the little ringed plover, which lacks a conspicuous white wingbar when seen in flight. Out on the water both little and great crested grebes breed. Autumn brings the possibility of passage waders. Check the pools visible from the bench and viewing area near Bouthwaite where, even if a greenshank or green sandpiper can't be found, the intricate plumage of the snipe can often be seen well.

Gouthwaite's reputation amongst birdwatchers is based primarily on the diversity of birds of prey seen there in the winter months. Birders gather at the viewpoint near Colt House along the western edge of the reservoir and put in many hours scanning the distant ridges for raptors. This walk involves a more dynamic approach, though you will maximise your chances if you have strategic stops to scan for birds of prey. Scan the area of heather moorland visible to your right as you approach Wath and the gill beyond Colville House.

Westerly winds and decent visibility are important conditions for raptor watching but even then a bit of luck is always needed. Buzzard, sparrowhawk and kestrel are regularly seen, with merlin and peregrine both fairly frequently recorded. An impressive list of rarities has been seen here in the winter months, most notably the awesome duo of white-tailed and golden eagles. The white-tailed eagle, or the 'flying barn door' as it is often described due to its massive two metre wingspan, was probably a one off but the reservoir did have a run of golden eagles in consecutive years. There hasn't been one of these jaw-dropping birds for a few years now so one may be due soon. A hen harrier is a more likely reward for a winter excursion and is always a pulse-quickening sight. Hen harriers have a dire breeding record on the grouse moors in the area due to illegal persecution but in the winter months numbers are boosted by birds dispersing into the Dales from Scotland and the continent. With rough-legged buzzard also seen here occasionally in winter, the birdwatcher has all the motivation needed for a walk through Nidderdale on a crisp winter's day.

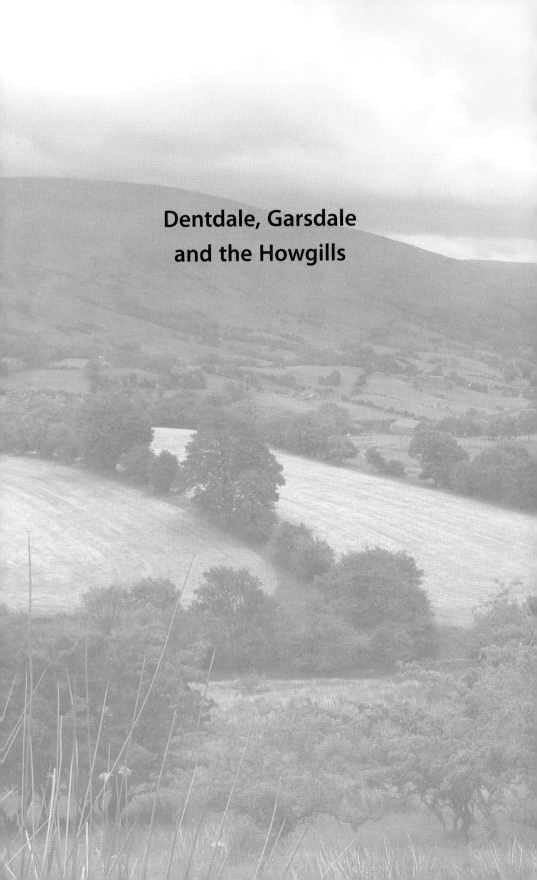

Dentdale, Garsdale
and the Howgills

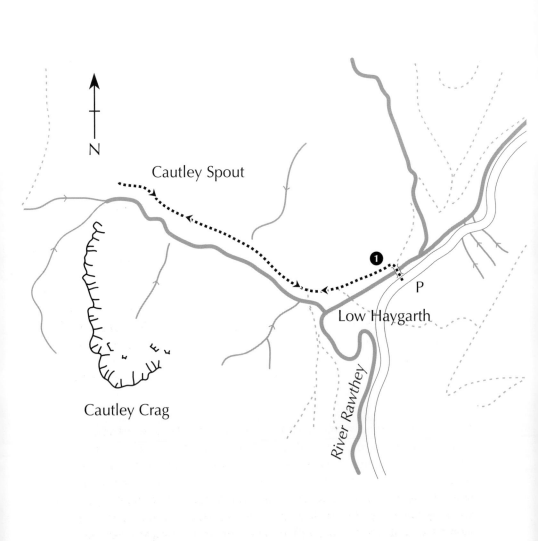

Cautley Spout

Cautley Crag

Low Haygarth

River Rawthey

N

P

Cautley

Birding around Cautley Spout

Stonechat

Length: 5.5 km (3.5 miles)
Time: Allow 2 hours
Season: March to July
Terrain/grade: Easy (but with an optional steep ascent)
Start: Free parking in layby after the Cross Keys. This is off the A683 linking Sedbergh and Kirkby Stephen, SD698969
Bus/train: The 564 Monday to Saturday bus service runs from Kirkby Stephen to Kendal via Sedbergh and stops at the Cross Keys
General: Refreshments at Cross Keys temperance inn

W ATERFALLS AND GOOD BIRDWATCHING can fortunately be combined at several places in the Yorkshire Dales and this walk provides a chance to see a range of interesting birds whilst admiring England's highest waterfall. The Howgills are visited comparatively rarely by walkers and birdwatchers alike, yet they provide a beautiful setting to see appealing Dales birds like peregrine falcon and dipper.

❶ **Take the footpath 90 m (100 yards) past the inn signed to Cautley Spout. Cross the bridge and then continue on this clear path as it takes you towards the bottom of the waterfall. Bear left when the path splits and use the path climbing up the right-hand side of the waterfall. (The energetic could consider extending the walk by following the beck above the waterfall and heading to the summit of Calders to your left or The Calf to your right.) Retrace your steps back to the Cross Keys.**

The River Rawthey with Cautley Crag in the distance

ⓘ The bridge over the River Rawthey is a good place to check for dipper
and grey wagtail. Dippers can be seen here all year round, though be
sure to scan the rocks and river fairly carefully as it is possible to miss
this characterful semi-aquatic bird. Sand martins arrive from early April
to breed in the river banks, though they can be thwarted by heavy
rainfall in spring and summer which washes their nesting burrows out.
As you head towards Cautley Spout check the areas of bracken and
the scattered rocks on the hillsides. Stonechats are usually obliging
in these bracken areas, whilst wheatears arrive in March and make a
pleasant sight with their smart plumage. Meadow pipits are numerous
in the area and the well-known song of the declining skylark can be
heard here.

Before reaching the waterfall your attention is likely to be drawn to the wide and imposing Cautley Crag to your left. It is worth spending some time scanning the crag and ridge, with a telescope coming in handy. The bulky raven is a regular sight. Ravens lay eggs early in the spring so that the young hatch around lambing time, ensuring a plentiful supply of carrion from the sheep that perish then. Look out for a peregrine falcon as well, sat high on the crag surveying the area. Peregrines are at their most impressive when hunting, when they climb high and then swoop at high speed onto their prey. Buzzards should also be seen here and you might be fortunate enough to see an altercation between any of the grand trio of buzzard, peregrine and raven. With the 180-metre (600-foot) series of drops of Cautley Spout ahead there can be few better theatres for such a birdwatching spectacle.

Raven

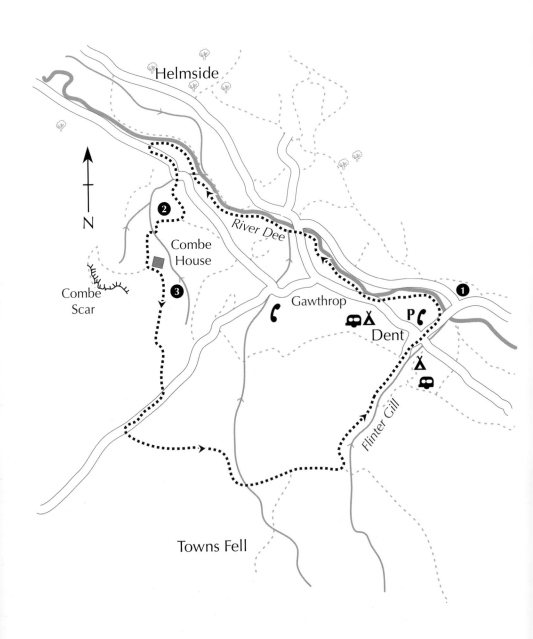

Helmside

River Dee

2

Combe
House

3

Combe
Scar

Gawthrop

1

P

Dent

Flinter Gill

Towns Fell

N

Dent

Redpolls and redstarts in Dentdale

Redstart

Length: 11 km (7 miles)
Time: Around 5 hours
Season: April to August
Terrain/grade: Moderate
Start: Dent village National Park car park, SD703872
Bus/train: Bus service 564 A/B connecting Dent to Sedbergh and Kendal currently runs only very infrequently on Wednesdays and Saturdays. Dent station is on the main Leeds to Carlisle line but be aware that it is 6.4 km (4 miles) east of Dent (though on Saturdays the bus does run from the station to the village)
General: Pubs and cafés in Dent, toilet block by car park

THIS IS A SUPERB walk through picturesque Dentdale. The birdlife matches the views here, with this walk offering an excellent chance to see two particularly attractive birds – the redpoll and the redstart.

❶ Turn left out of the car park and cross the cobbled streets, bearing left downhill when the road splits. Head to the bridge across the Dee, and take the footpath left just before the bridge. Follow this path along the riverside before coming to the road. Turn right onto it for a short time and then take a right by a wooden bench with a signpost for Barth Bridge. Continue on this path to Barth Bridge where you need to cross the road and take the footpath straight ahead. Follow this path as it keeps close to the riverside before winding off left to the road after around a mile. Turn left onto the quiet road and follow it for a

Dentdale from the hillside above Combe House – the bushes in the foreground are
excellent for tree pipit, redpoll and redstart in the spring and summer

short distance. After the road winds left take a right by the farm, signed Bower Bank/Stone Rigg.

❶ As you pass through the cobbled streets of Dent you will notice the granite monument on your left dedicated to Dent's most famous son, Adam Sedgwick. Sedgwick was born in the village in 1785 and went on to become one of the founding fathers of modern geology, befriending Queen Victoria and disagreeing with Charles Darwin in the process. Difficult as it is to leave the picturesque streets behind, the river provides a lure with its wealth of birdlife. Both dippers and goosanders can be seen throughout the year, whilst spring sees the arrival of the common sandpipers that bob up and down on the rocks. In the summer look out for a family of grey wagtails with the colourless juveniles being fed by the brighter parents. Sand martins always provide entertainment by performing their aerial acrobatics over the water's edge, and the fortunate might see a kingfisher flash by giving its sharp whistle. In the stretch of river after Barth Bridge attention can turn to the birds that define this walk in the spring and summer months, the redpoll and the redstart. Check the hedges on your left-hand side for the red tail of a redstart as it darts into cover, and be alert for the buzzing song flight of the redpoll overhead as it moves agitatedly from bush to bush.

❷ **The track soon turns left uphill and then bears right uphill towards a ruin. After the ruin, the track runs out into a poorly marked grassy path. Aim uphill for the top left-hand corner of the field past the ruin and go through a metal gate to reach a track. Turn right onto the track and continue to Tofts. Enter Tofts and head between the buildings to a small wooden gate directly ahead. Descend the steps and cross a small bridge over the stream. From here follow the few waymarker posts to join a track and head uphill towards Combe House. Head past the left hand side of the house and take the grassy path bearing left between a fence and a drystone wall.**

❶ The climb up towards Combe Scar can seem tough work, with fewer birds than the riverside and often only the views across the beautiful Dentdale to spur the legs on. The reward for the effort comes with an avian feast around Combe House in the spring and summer months that is not to be missed. The fighter jet of the skies, the peregrine falcon, and the hardy raven preside over the wealth of smaller birds below from the heights of the scar. Listen for the distinctive mewing call of the buzzard as it passes overhead. The area of scattered hawthorns and ash you reach by passing through the gate after Combe House is packed with *Passerines* and is where a birdwatching walk should slow down dramatically in pace! The featured birds of the walk, the redstart and the redpoll, both find this area a perfect habitat and can be seen at close quarters without the difficulties that can be encountered trying to locate them in woodland. They must rank as two of the most attractive species in the Dales, with the brilliant orange, grey and black plumage of the male redstart and distinctive red breast and forehead of the redpoll a joy to see.

Tree pipit

Though these two birds might threaten to steal the birding show, this is an area that proves attractive for an excellent selection of other species. Tree pipits can be heard at the bottom of the scar and in the stretch of hillside bushes after Combe House. Be careful over identification as meadow pipits also occur here and also perch in the hawthorns. Look for the more marked supercilium (stripe above the eye) and thicker bill of the tree pipit. The well-defined breast streaking which sharply becomes very fine and indistinct on the flanks is another good identification feature. Willow warbler are present in numbers and can dominate the chorus of bird song here in the spring. The pied flycatcher can also be seen, confirming that this area is woodland birdwatching made easy!

❸ Continue on the path through a metal gate and along the hillside before it loops round left. Aim for a stile in the bottom right-hand corner of the boggy field. The path is faint among the limestone boulders thereafter but bear right along the wall for 20 m (22 yards) and then bear left as the path moves up through the limestone boulders. Follow the path to the road and then turn right and walk on it for a few hundred metres before taking a path on your left signed to Dent. Continue on this path and then take the left hand path down Flinter Gill, also signed to Dent. At the bottom of the gill follow the road straight down, keeping the playground on your right and you are brought back to the car park.

❶ The next section of the walk traverses moorland and gives views of the steep ridge which peaks at Calf Top and the upper end of Barbondale. This is good wheatear country as they perch atop limestone boulders and drystone walls. Meadow pipits can seem abundant and a few skylark accompany you. These small birds might prove an irresistible draw to a merlin speeding low over the moorland. Be prepared for inhospitable weather here, particularly in winter when the birdwatcher might find few birds save for an occasional raven or even hen harrier. Descending down Flinter Gill gives a chance of more woodland birds, though they can be difficult to see here. You can even make a wish by passing underneath the wishing tree to your right as you near the end of the gill!

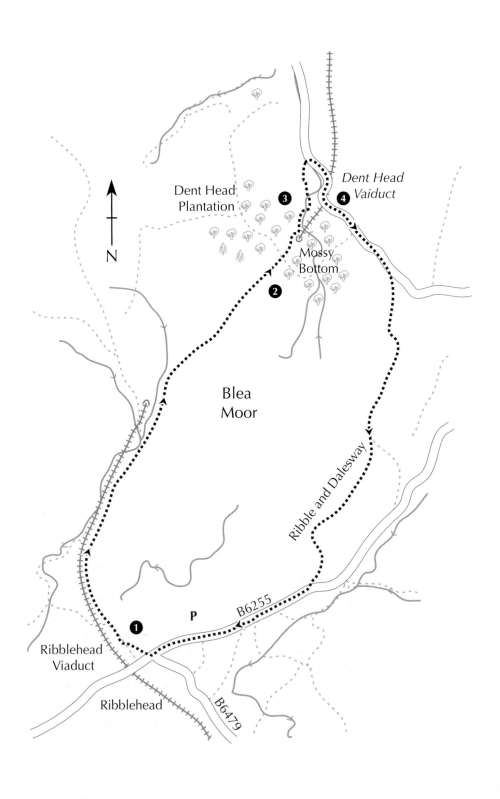

N

Dent Head
Plantation

3

Dent Head
Vaiduct

4

Mossy
Bottom

2

Blea
Moor

Ribble and Dalesway

1

P   B6255

Ribblehead
Viaduct

Ribblehead

B6479

Ribblehead

Crossbills and viaducts

Dent Head Viaduct

Length: 13 km (8 miles)
Time: Around 5 hours
Season: All year: March to May probably best
Terrain/grade: Moderate
Start: Ribblehead, plenty of free parking by side of
B6255, SD768795
Bus/train: Ribblehead station is on the main Leeds to
Carlisle line
General: The Station Inn and snack van at Ribblehead
provide refreshment

ALTHOUGH THE FOCUS OF this book is on the delights of the natural world, this walk also offers the opportunity to marvel at the feats of man in the Dales. Three impressive viaducts punctuate the walk, including the famous Ribblehead Viaduct with its twenty four arches standing around a hundred foot high. Drawing the walker back to the natural world are the appealing crossbills that have colonised the conifers overlooking Dent Head Viaduct.

❶ **Walk along the road to the T junction between the B6255 and the B6479. Opposite this is a grassy path signed for Blea Moor Sidings which you need to take. Turn right shortly after onto a stone track and then bear right off this track shortly before it heads underneath the viaduct. Head uphill following this path, signed for Whernside, and continue as it skirts the eastern edge of the railway line. Not long after the signal box, and with a wooden footbridge over the stream visible ahead, you need to turn right onto the track leading uphill towards the spoil heaps. Head between the spoils, over a stile and continue on the grassy path over Blea Moor.**

ⓘ The magnificent Ribblehead Viaduct dominates the opening section of the walk. It was constructed between 1870 and 1875 by an army of several thousand workers, or 'navvies', who lived in shanty towns adjacent to the viaduct. The harsh weather conditions in this notoriously exposed place took their toll on the workers. Gambling and drinking were the favoured leisure pursuits of the men and one navvy is even said to have sold his wife for a barrel of beer! The construction work was dangerous in itself but it was outbreaks of smallpox that ensured an especially high death toll during the five years. The graveyard at Chapel-le-Dale had to be extended and a memorial to the workers who lost their lives can be seen at St Leonard's Church.

Thankfully the hardest task for the birdwatcher here now is trying to figure out how many stonechats there are in the area. Look out for this species as you walk alongside the viaduct as it can often give excellent views here. The male stonechat is a fine specimen with his orange breast and prominent white collar. Ravens are present in the general area and you may hear its deep, rolling call overhead. As you climb up towards Blea Moor, you pass the lonely signal boxes and begin to climb up with the 2.4 km (2,629 yard) long Blea Moor Tunnel beneath you. The tunnel was constructed at the same time as the viaduct by candlelight and the spoil heaps you pass through still hint at the scale of the task undertaken. Meadow pipits are commonplace and kestrels hover over the slopes. Merlins breed in the area and watching one in pursuit of a hapless meadow pipit is enough to enthrall even the most experienced birdwatcher. The decline of the skylark has been well documented but fortunately the famous song of this species still fills the air on Blea Moor.

ⓚ ❷ Continue past a chimney and downhill towards a gap in the forest. Head over the stile and descend, crossing the track in front and continuing to descend as signed.

ⓘ Look north from the vantage point of Blea Moor to see another viaduct, the Arten Gill Viaduct, which is actually taller than Ribblehead Viaduct at 35.6 m (117 feet) high. At Dent Head Plantation birdwatching is to the fore, with the crossbills providing an irresistible draw. Scan from the higher ground of Blea Moor to check for these super finches and then be alert as you descend through the conifers for the loud and repeated 'chip chip' calls of the birds as they rove through the plantation. Crossbills are unusual for starting their long breeding cycle very early, meaning you can see juvenile birds as early as February and March. Siskins are also present here in good numbers and complement the more usual residents such as goldcrests and coal tits. The nocturnal long-eared owl breeds in some years but this species really requires an early morning or late evening visit.

❶ ❸ Take the path past Blea Moor Tunnel to a farmyard. Pass through the wooden gate and then bear left in the farmyard to cross over the beck. Continue on this path and shortly after a wooden gate turn right over a grassy topped bridge with a house opposite.

❶ Make sure you stop when you finally reach the end of the tunnel for this is a terrific area for wild flowers, particularly orchids. Common spotted orchids cover the area and you might pick out a frog orchid amongst them. The rare small pearl-bordered fritillary, on the wing in June and the first week of July and best located on sunny days, has also been recorded. Roe deer can be fairly regularly encountered in the Dent Head area and always cut a majestic figure. As you move towards the road and away from the plantation look for great spotted woodpecker and redstart in the woodland and be prepared for some amazing-looking chickens and guineafowl in the farmyard you pass through!

❹ Turn right onto the road and continue under the viaduct and up the hill past the forest. Where the road begins to level out look for a path on your right signed to the B6255. Take this track for around 2 km (1.5 miles) before turning right as the path begins to descend slightly by the sign for Gearstones. Keep on the path, which descends as the wall on your left-hand side drops down. By the house, bear right on the lane that drops down to the road. Returning on the road can be worrying as traffic can move at high speeds so it is best to take advantage of the new access rights and walk along the edge of the hillside skirting the road. There is a faint path you might be able to pick up where people have done this and this takes you back to Ribblehead. Be careful here as there are shake holes (steep-sided hole or dip where the ground falls into underground holes) and boggy areas, so keep near to the road if in any doubt.

❶ Walking underneath Dent Head Viaduct helps give an impression of the scale of this huge 109 m (119 yard) long structure. As you climb up the hill there is a magnificent picture-perfect view of the viaduct with the fells and Dentdale in the background. Scan Wold Fell to your left for buzzard and raven. In the winter months wandering peregrines and hen harrier are both possible. As you leave the road and head back to Ribblehead, curlew and lapwing should be much in evidence and a beautiful short-eared owl might be seen hunting actively for voles over the moor. Good views of skylark and wheatears might be had near Ribblehead before well-deserved rest and refreshment beckons at the Station Inn.

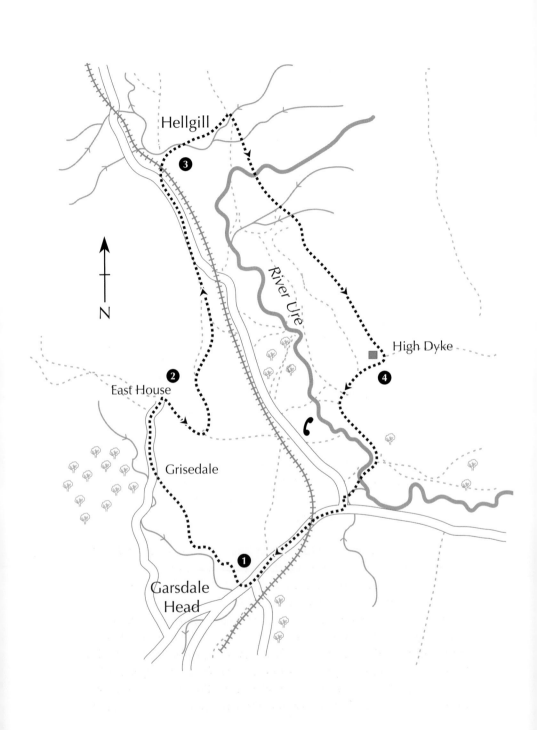

Garsdale

Snipe along the four valleys walk

Snipe

Length: Around 14 km (8.5 miles)
Time: Allow 6 hours
Season: April to August
Terrain/grade: Moderate
Start: Garsdale station. There is parking here but getting the train along the famous Settle to Carlisle section is highly recommended, SD789918
Bus/train: Garsdale station is on the main Leeds–Carlisle railway line. Harrogate and District Community Transport buses run infrequently from Hawes to the station (Monday to Saturday)
General: Refreshments at the Moorcock Inn

THIS WALK OFFERS THE beautiful and varied scenery of four different valleys. The fantastic foursome are Garsdale, its tributary valley Grisedale, Maller-stang and the head of Wensleydale. Featured amongst the wide range of birds to be seen is the cryptic snipe.

❶ Turn right out of the station and take the minor road heading north. At the junction with the main road, look for the small wooden gate opposite. The path through this field is faint but bear right slightly and continue uphill to a stile about 25 m (30 yards) right of a wooden gate. The faint path soon takes you away from the views over the beck and heads towards the farmhouse at Blake Mire. Aim for a metal gate 45 m (50 yards) beyond the house on your left but be careful as the ground is often boggy here. In the next field aim to the left of the barn visible ahead and then, after passing this, aim in the direction

of 1 o'clock to reach a gap in the wall. Descend to the ruined barn and bear left. Continue on the track to the metal gate and then turn right onto the quiet lane. Follow the lane up past East House and through the metal gate.

ⓘ The wild and remote nature of this walk means there are birds as soon as you step off the train. Sparrowhawks soar above the conifer plantation by the platform and the fortunate might encounter the elusive long-eared owl at dusk or dawn. As you continue on to Grisedale, you are entering the hidden valley that was the subject of the film *The Dale that Died*. This was once a busy farming community of over a dozen families and with a reputation for religious nonconformity through early Quaker and later Methodist meetings. The economic depression of the 1930s saw the beginning of the 'death' of the dale. Only one farming family was left by the time of the film in 1975. Now the dale lives again thanks partly to refurbishment for holiday homes. Nevertheless it remains a gloriously isolated place often shrouded by mist and cloud in the winter months. In spring the oystercatchers return to the beck and sand martins arrive to breed in the banks. Few birdwatchers ever venture here but the area is full of potential. There are black grouse in the area and the conifer plantations provide habitat for crossbills and even an occasional pair of long-eared owl.

🚶 ❷ Keep on the track as it veers right and then turn right when it splits. A path is marked on the map heading up the hillside towards Mallerstang but there is no path on the ground. It's probably best to keep on the track heading south-east and then bearing left a little to hit the drystone wall with a wooden stile at the far end of the field. Don't go over the stile, instead turn left and follow the wall up the hillside. When the wall ends and is replaced by a fence you need to turn right through the metal gate to pick up the path heading to Aisgill. Head at about 11 o'clock along this faint path as it takes you out at a small stream. Bear left with the path and aim for High Shaw Paddock ahead, keeping roughly on the same level. You pass through a rushy area, which can be boggy after wet weather, and reach a wooden gate before the barn. Head through a gap in the wall to skirt the right-hand side of the barn and then pass through the metal gate. The path then keeps fairly straight alongside the wall before descending right just before the cottages to the road.

Hell Gill Force – a hidden waterfall near the source of the River Eden

ℹ As you continue up past East House, lapwing and curlew, which arrive in early spring, should both be prominent. Snipe breed in the rushy areas here and over the brow in Mallerstang. On a calm spring morning the birdwatcher might see the amazing drumming display of this wader, where a bleating noise is made by the sound of the wind rushing through the outer tail feathers of the bird. As you cross over into Mallerstang you enter another good area for breeding waders. The alarm cries of the lapwings act as a useful guide to the birder because they might signify the presence of a bird of prey. A merlin is a real highlight of any Dales walk and can be seen here moving fast and purposefully over the lower slopes of Swarth Fell. You have a good chance of seeing short-eared owls early in the morning on the moors to your left as you approach Aisgill Moor Cottages. These moors are also worth checking for the black grouse, which still maintains a tenuous hold here.

❸ Cross the road and turn left onto it before taking a right signed Hell Gill. Cross the railway bridge and follow this track for about 100 m (110 yards) then bear right before the stream (Hell Gill Force is just off to your left). Follow the path up past the farm and cross Hell Gill Bridge on your right to pick up the High Way. Soon you will need to bear left when the path forks and then

follow the clear track for nearly 3 km (2 miles) before you reach a ruined house at High Dyke on your right.

ⓘ At Aisgill moor cottages the famous Settle–Carlisle railway line reaches its highest point at 356.3 m (1169 feet) above sea level (see also Walk 19). The bridge over the railway line is a good place to scan the scattered bushes on the embankment for the redpolls which breed here. As you continue it is worth stopping at the lovely Hell Gill Force. Looking down into the waterfall with mistle thrushes and goldcrests in the trees above can provide the perfect mid-walk break.

The next section of the walk takes you past Hell Gill Bridge to the east and west boundary between the source of the River Eden and the source of the River Ure. You are now on the High Way, travelled by Lady Anne Clifford in the seventeenth century as she sought to rebuild the northern castles she had gained after a long inheritance battle. Look for the yellow and orange of 'eggs and bacon', or bird's foot trefoil as it is officially known, whilst the powerful raven glides overhead. This is a good track for birds of prey that use the updraft from westerly winds to glide across the ridge. Buzzards are common and the intricate variations of their plumage can be seen unusually well here. Kestrel and sparrowhawk are regularly seen whilst the optimistic might hope for an osprey using the valley as a migration route to and from Scotland.

🚶 ❹ **Turn right shortly after the house at High Dyke through a metal gate and then descend straight down the hill. In the third field down bear left at about 11 o'clock along a faint path to Blades. Head over the stile and through the metal gate and then after only 50 m (55 yards) head left over another stile. Turn left when you reach the clear track and follow this path as it heads alongside the River Ure (ignore the first bridge off to your right). Cross the next bridge over the Ure and then bear left in the direction of the Moorcock Inn. From here you need to walk for a short distance along the road back to the junction at Garsdale Head where you turn left and return to the station.**

ⓘ As you descend to Blades Farm look for stonechat which breed in the rushy areas around the farm. The path along the River Ure past the farm is excellent for breeding waders in the spring, with snipe, lapwing, oystercatcher, redshank and curlew making a wonderful spectacle. With grey wagtail and dipper possible near the bridge the birder can head back to the Moorcock Inn happy.

Wensleydale, Swaledale and Arkengarthdale

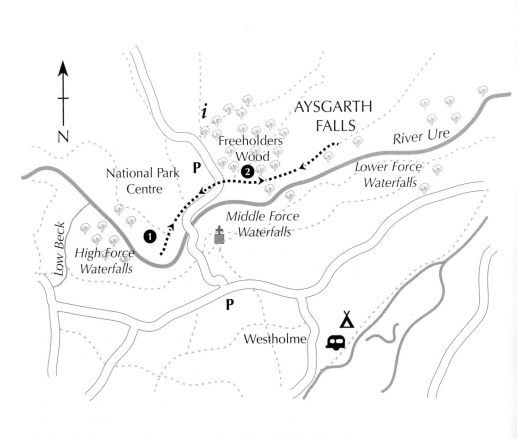

N

AYSGARTH
FALLS

River Ure

i

Freeholders
Wood

P

❷

Lower Force
Waterfalls

National Park
Centre

❶

*Middle Force
Waterfalls*

Low Beck

*High Force
Waterfalls*

P

Westholme

Aysgarth

Dippers for all the family

Dipper

Length: 1.5 km (1 mile)
Time: 1 hour
Season: All year
Terrain/grade: Easy
Start: National Park pay and display car park near Aysgarth Falls, SE012887
Bus/train: The 156 Dales and District bus service runs between Northallerton and Hawes and stops at Aysgarth (Monday to Saturday). For access to the falls, the best stop is opposite the minor road leading to the National Park Centre
General: Toilets and refreshments at the tourist information centre by the car park

No WALKER OR BIRDWATCHER can always get away with leaving family or friends at home while they hike around the Dales. This walk tries to offer a compromise solution. It is a short and easy stroll to view the renowned and superb Aysgarth Falls. With dippers diving heartily into the Ure by the falls hopefully everyone can go home happy!

❶ The Upper Falls can be viewed by taking the path left at the end of the car park furthest away from the information centre. Follow this to a picnic area by the river (there is an honesty box here asking for a small donation).

❶ The Upper Falls at Aysgarth might seem familiar to film fans as they were the setting for Robin Hood's fight with Little John in the film *Robin Hood: Prince of Thieves*. Early mornings here are a good time to see the ever popular kingfisher perched on an overhanging branch or

Aysgarth Lower Falls

flying speedily downstream. The Upper Falls area should produce good views of dipper perched on a rock or half submerged under the water 'swimming' for insect larvae. This beguiling bird is always fantastic value to watch and can be seen at any time of year. Grey wagtails should also be seen on the Ure. In spring and summer large numbers of swifts, swallows, house and sand martins hawk for insects over the river.

(🚶) ❷ **Retrace your steps back through the car park and pick up the path past the centre. Follow this as it bears round right and then cross the road. Bear right after passing through the gate on the path signed Lower and Middle Falls. Follow this path, with steep steps leading down to the viewing platform for the Middle Falls on your right-hand side. The path does a small loop past a viewing area for the Lower Falls and then returns you back to the car park.**

(ℹ) The woodland area you pass through holds a good variety of resident species, including great spotted woodpecker, treecreeper and nuthatch. Spring sees the arrival of blackcap and garden warbler. They can both be seen well from the path leading to the Middle and Lower Falls. Look for spotted flycatcher too which arrive in early May and make dashes for insects from branches or fences. The Lower Falls area provides another excellent spot for dipper and grey wagtail. Check the skies for buzzards which are now frequently seen in the area and return to the centre for some refreshment and a display on the social and natural history of the area.

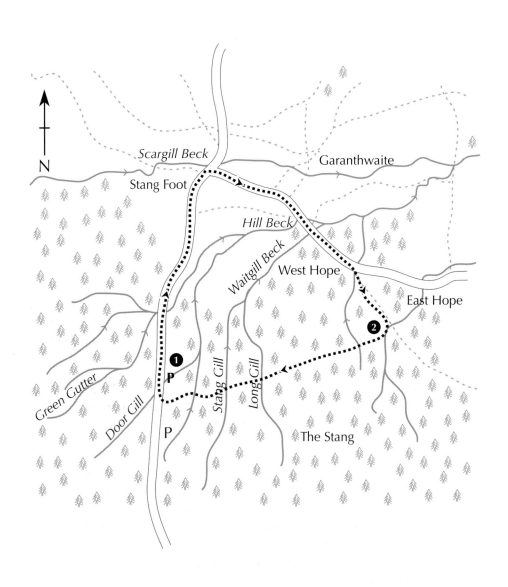

Scargill Beck

Garanthwaite

Stang Foot

Hill Beck

Waitgill Beck

West Hope

East Hope

Green Gutter

Door Gill

Stang Gill

Long Gill

The Stang

N

1

P

P

2

The Stang

Hawks and doves around The Stang

Goshawk

Length: 4 km (2.5 miles)
Time: Allow 2 hours
Season: All year
Terrain/grade: Easy
Start: Murker Hill free car park, NZ024087
Bus/train: None available
General: No refreshments available

T HIS WALK TAKES YOU just over the county border into Durham and explores the sprawling coniferous forest of The Stang. It is a real birdwatcher's walk, lacking the fantastic scenery of many others in this guide but making up for it by offering a selection of scarce and exciting birds.

❶ **Turn right out of the car park and walk carefully along Stang Lane to Stang Foot. At Stang Foot take the lane right signed to Hope. Continue along the lane through West Hope and then climb a hill.**

ⓘ Don't be in a rush to leave the car park as good birds can often be seen in the immediate vicinity. Tree pipits arrive in spring and perform their song flight landing onto the tree tops whilst chiffchaffs and blackcaps sing heartily. Heading out of the forest be alert for an encounter with the superbly colourful turtle dove. The forest edge and Stang Foot area have provided sightings of this stunningly exotic looking bird in recent years. The birds can be shy but listen out for their distinctive and deep purring song. Collared doves are normally around Stang Lodge and woodpigeons are common in the area. Stock doves can usually be seen around the barn on your right-hand side as you approach Stang Foot.

Goshawk   M°7

The area of farmland alongside the lane heading towards West
Hope provides a different habitat. Swallows breed in the barns in the
summer whilst linnets perch on telegraph wires. The yaffle of the green
woodpecker might be heard and this is a very good area for tawny owl,
though their appearances are usually limited to the twilight hours. The
lane also provides a good place to scan the skies above the forest for
birds of prey. March and April are the best months for this, though
patience may be rewarded at any time of year. Buzzards are regularly
seen and healthy numbers of sparrowhawks are resident in the forest.
Be alert for the possibility of its rarer and more powerful cousin, the
goshawk, in the early spring. Look for the weightier build and longer
wingspan of the goshawk, which also has a broader-based tail with
rounded corners.

**② As the lane levels out ignore the stone track leading off to your
right and take the next path right shortly after a public bridleway
sign. After a few hundred metres you reach a more open area
with rushes to your right. Here turn right onto the stone track
and head west back to the road. Continue along the track as it
maintains a straight line, ignoring the first track leading left and
the stone tracks branching off right. Return to the road and turn
right over the small bridge to reach the car park.**

❶ Moving into the area of dense Sitka Spruce forest the density of birds
becomes thinner, though the quality makes up for this. Goldcrests
are present in large numbers with their short and very high pitched
calls usually betraying their presence. As you turn off the main lane
and head west on the track through the forest you have a chance of
seeing crossbills. They are present throughout the year and a sighting
of a bright red male with its hefty powerful bill is not easily forgotten.
Gorgeous finches are a feature of the walk, with redpoll, siskin and the
more chunky bullfinch all adding a splash of colour to the forest. If
you are walking on a late summer evening you might hear a different
selection of species, with the 'squeaky gates' of young long-eared owls,
the grunting of woodcocks and even the churring of a male nightjar all
possible. The Stang may require a little patience and persistence but
there are many irresistible birds here to lure the birdwatcher.

Crossbill

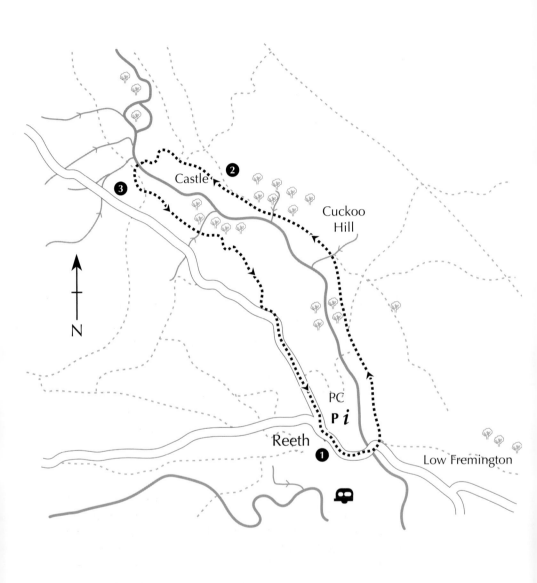

N

Castle

Cuckoo
Hill

PC

P *i*

Reeth

Low Fremington

① ② ③

Reeth

The two flycatchers walk

Pied flycatcher

Length:	Around 6 km (4 miles)
Time:	2.5 to 3 hours
Season:	Late April to August, though the visit needs to be in May or June to see both species of flycatcher.
Terrain/grade:	Easy
Start:	Reeth village green, small sum payable by honesty box, SE038993
Bus/train:	Buses run by Harkers, G Abbott and Sons and Harrogate District Community Transport from Richmond stop at Reeth village green (Monday to Saturday)
General:	Refreshments in Reeth. A toilet block is adjacent to the north end of the village green. The Swaledale Folk Museum is well worth a visit and is signed from the eastern end of the village green

REETH HAS BEEN A bustling and interesting market town for centuries and this walk gives a chance to see a wealth of birdlife within a short circular route of this popular base. The highlight of the walk is the chance to see both species of flycatcher that breed in Britain. For those interested in theatre and music, timing a visit to coincide with the excellent Swaledale Festival in late May and early June would provide a feast of both birds and culture.

❶ Bear left downhill from Reeth village green and cross the bridge over the Arkle. Take the first left after the bridge and head along the track. After passing straight through a couple of fields bear right up the mound and pass through the gap in the

wall on your right. Keep left along the fence and up to a metal gate. Follow the path as it drops down and then moves away from the river into woodland.

❶ The River Arkle never becomes more than a large stream before it joins the Swale near Grinton yet it still hosts a wealth of wildlife. It is worth pausing near the bridge to check the river. A kingfisher might zoom past uttering its high-pitched whistle and you might even be able to find signs of the presence of the elusive otter. It is the woodland species, though, that are likely to prove the stars of this walk. The first area of woodland on your left, as well as the trees lining the walls on your right, can produce both pied flycatcher and redstart. As the path drops down to the river, stop to look for dipper and grey wagtail before your attention turns again to the woodland specialities. Climbing up into a wooded area you pass through a gap in the wall with an ash tree ahead. Pied flycatchers still regularly use the nestbox here and pausing at a respectful distance can allow study of this terrific bird.

❷ After passing through the main area of woodland, bear left when the path splits (on the footpath rather than bridleway). Bear left slightly after Castle Farm House to a track that then curves down to a bridge over the Arkle.

❶ As you skirt the hillside listen for the familiar sound of the cuckoo in spring. There is a certain symmetry here in hearing a cuckoo on the slopes of Cuckoo Hill! The main woodland area alongside the river is an excellent spot for birds and should be carefully checked. Nuthatch is common along with a good selection of resident species including the scarce marsh tit. In spring the woods really come to life, with the descending trills of willow warblers and the melodies of blackcaps filling the air. Both the flycatcher species, pied and spotted, occur here in close proximity and might be seen in quick succession on a May or June visit. The subtlety and character of the spotted flycatcher is complemented well by the distinctive black and white plumage of the male pied flycatcher. Spotted flycatchers have seriously declined across much of Britain but they are thankfully still a common sight in Arkengarthdale in the summer months. As you continue, listen out for the yaffle of the wonderful green woodpecker and look for the bounding flight and pied plumage of the great spotted woodpecker. Redstarts perch on the walls of the disused barn on your right as you approach Castle Farm.

(✻) ❸ **Cross the bridge and then follow the path through a wooden gate after it turns left uphill. Pass through a metal gate and shortly after, with a barn to your right, turn left onto a faint grassy path. Please walk single file in this section of the walk to protect the hay meadows on either side. The path keeps fairly straight and level, though bear right slightly to cross a small stream at the end of a fenced-off area. The stiles are marked with yellow paint on the wall and it is a matter of following these before the path bears right and brings you out onto the road. Turn left onto the road and follow it for the short distance back to Reeth.**

❶ At the bridge check the river for dipper. The woodland here is good for nuthatch all year and spotted flycatcher in the spring and summer. The fenceposts to your left as you climb the hill are a regular perch for the spotted flycatcher. Goldfinches abound on the walk back to Reeth but the birdwatcher should check the area carefully for the much rarer twite. A few pairs of this fast-disappearing finch still breed on the Arkengarthdale moors and if you are lucky they can be seen feeding at the top end of the hay meadows before you turn left onto the path towards Reeth. As you head back towards the town, kestrels can afford fine views of their beautiful plumage to provide a pleasing finale. Reeth may not quite be as bustling a place as it used to be, with records from 1890 showing two watchmakers and no fewer than six boot- and shoemakers plying their trade in the town, but it is still a pleasant market town to explore and enjoy.

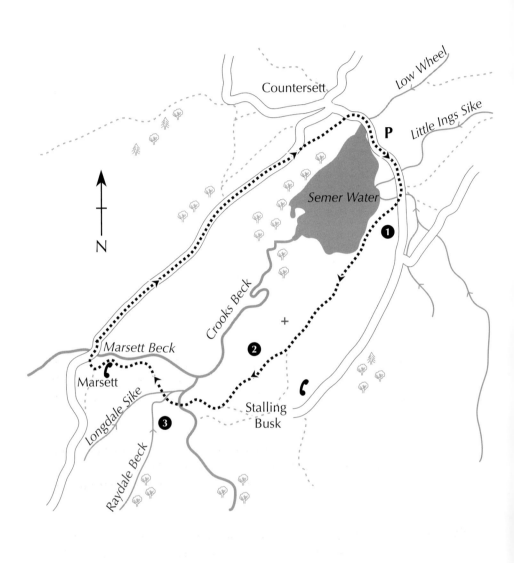

Semer Water

Ducks and deer at Semer Water

Semer Water

Length: 6.5 km (4 miles)

Time: Allow 3 hours

Season: All year

Terrain/grade: Easy

Start: Parking available on the north-eastern shore of the lake, SD 923876. Tickets can be bought at nearby Low Blean Farm

Bus/train: None available, nearest stop at Bainbridge 5 km (3 miles) away

General: Nearest refreshments/toilets at Bainbridge

Semer Water is a wonderfully tranquil natural lake and a fantastic setting with distinctive Addleborough watching proudly over it to the east. The winter months bring an influx of ducks, whilst roe deer are unusually visible throughout the year.

❶ Follow the road down towards Low Blean Farm and then take the path right just after the stream (signed to Stalling Busk). Follow this path, parallel to the lake shore, to the chapel on your right.

❶ Good views of the lake can be had from the first section of the walk. In autumn ducks return to the lake to spend the winter and normally include good numbers of wigeon and tufted duck. With teal, pochard and a few goldeneye also likely, the birdwatcher can get excellent views of a variety of wild ducks. Spring sees water levels fall and common sandpipers and oystercatchers return to breed on the shore. Watch out for the lost village of Simmerdale when the water levels drop; it is said to have been submerged by the lake after the curse of an old beggar who found no charity in the village. Great crested grebes display vigorously over the lost village in spring and occasionally a pair of wigeon stay to breed. The spring or autumn passage periods could produce an occasional scarcity such as black tern or osprey. The ornithologist Charles Fothergill toured the area in 1805 and was sure that 'if Semer Water was only better regarded by a resident' it would doubtless 'afford many extremely rare and curious water birds'. More birdwatchers visiting the area could prove the observation correct over 200 years later!

❷ After the chapel, pass through a wooden gate and then bear right, signed to Marsett. Continue along this faint path in roughly the same direction, looking out for a small stile hidden just right of a gate. On reaching a barn to your right, ignore the path left leading uphill to Stalling Busk and instead bear right towards Crooks Beck.

Semer Water with Addleborough in the distance

❶ Semer Water might command attention but there is also plenty of wildlife lurking in the bushes and meadows. Redpolls and willow warblers breed, whilst kestrels hunt the fields near the chapel. After admiring the chapel, which dates back to 1722 and is now ruined, look across towards the woodland bordering Crooks Beck for roe deer. Normally views of deer are of the back end as they run away from you but here you can observe them through binoculars at a comfortable distance.

(🚶) **❸ Cross the beck and turn right onto a track. Don't panic when you reach Raydale Beck and can't figure out how to cross it – there is a footbridge tucked away to your left! Follow the track to Marsett and then on reaching the village bear right on a grassy path to the bridge. Cross the bridge and follow the normally quiet lane up towards Carr End. Continue past the farm and the Old Silk Mill and then, as you begin to descend, look for a footpath off to your right signed to Semer Water Bridge. Follow the yellow-topped posts through the field and over the stream before taking a faint path leading through the edge of the wooded area. Take the gate visible ahead and turn right onto the road to return.**

❶ The remainder of the walk through peaceful Raydale is perfectly relaxing on a fine spring or summer's day. Look at the meadows as you cross the two becks as they are covered in flowers, including numerous common spotted orchids. The stunning kingfisher sometimes ventures up Crooks Beck after successfully catching a fish on Semer Water. On the lane back towards Semer Water Bridge there are good views of the lake, with Addleborough in the background. Look down on the shoreline where waders including lapwing, redshank and snipe can be seen. Check the scattered trees and bushes bordering the lane for woodland birds including redstarts. At Carr End, spotted flycatchers have taken recently to nesting in the eaves of the house. When returning to the car take one last look at the dead wood branches overhanging the north-west corner of the lake for a kingfisher. They have been seen on the lake for over two centuries, with Charles Fothergill noting how 'they fly out over Semer Water in the manner of the flycatcher'. Much has changed since this colourful ornithologist and journalist visited the Dales but some treasured birds remain to be appreciated into the twenty-first century.

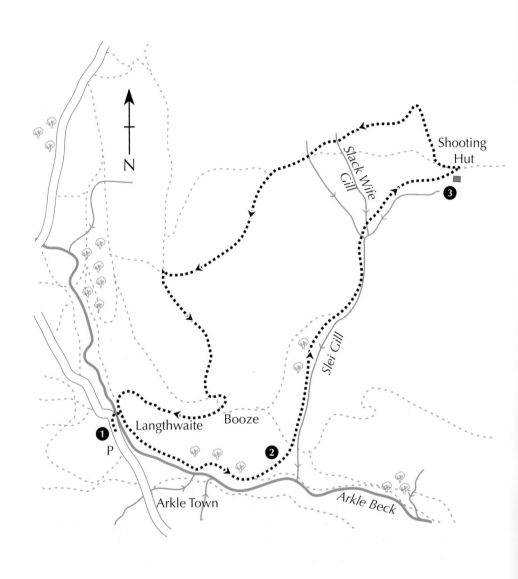

N

Shooting
Hut

Slack Wife Gill

Slei Gill

Langthwaite

Booze

1

P

2

3

Arkle Town

Arkle Beck

Langthwaite

The moorcock in Herriot Country

Red grouse

Length: 9 km (5.5 miles)
Time: Around 3 hours
Season: All year, best late March to June
Terrain/grade: Moderate
Start: Langthwaite pay and display car park, NZ005024
Bus/train: None currently available – nearest bus stop is in Reeth
General: Refreshments at the Red Lion, Langthwaite. Toilet block 150 m north west of car park

THIS WALK OFFERS WONDERFULLY varied scenery and birdlife in a dale that has changed little over the years. The walk takes you from the huddled cluster of houses in picturesque Langthwaite to the wilderness of Booze Moor above. The red grouse, or moorcock as it is known locally, is the characteristic bird of the heather moors. The Arkengarthdale moors provide an excellent chance to see this species at close range all year round.

❶ It is worth pointing out that navigation can be tricky on this walk so be prepared to take your time. Turn right out of the car park and then take the lane over the stone bridge across the Arkle. Turn right immediately after the bridge (opposite the Red Lion) to walk alongside the river. Continue on this track into the woodland where you should bear left following the sign for a bridleway, disregarding the sign for a footpath forking right.

❶ Langthwaite was made famous after featuring on the opening credits of the TV series *All Creatures Great and Small*. The series was based on the novels by James Herriot and it is easy to see why the television producers headed to Langthwaite for their well-known opening scene. It is a wonderfully picturesque village where the pace of life still remains far removed from the commotion of the towns. As you cross over the bridge and skirt the river, pause to look for dipper and grey wagtail. The woodland can be alive with birds in the spring. Great spotted woodpeckers are always a welcome sight and are seen here throughout the year. In spring blackcaps, chiffchaffs and willow warblers arrive and help to provide a fine dawn chorus. A tawny owl might still be visible in the early morning and a careful search could produce pied flycatcher and redstart. Goldcrests utter their very high pitched calls from the coniferous trees near the end of the woodland whilst the smart goldfinch is common throughout the area.

🚶 **❷ Pass through the wood and two gates, keeping straight on the track signed Slei Gill. At the next fork in the path continue straight ahead again on the flat grassy path. Pass between the two left-hand most spoil heaps as the path becomes indistinct and continue up the gill. At the head of the gill, the path crosses the small beck and then heads north but becomes faint and difficult to follow. Aim just to the left of the wooden shooting hut ahead and join a stone track.**

🛈 The scattered bushes at the start of Slei Gill hold redstart and spotted flycatcher in the spring and summer as well as the more expected 'charms' of goldfinch. Small birds need to be alert as sparrowhawks regularly hunt the area. Sparrowhawks can be surprisingly elusive even if several pairs are breeding locally, but they make an impressive sight when seen well, with their fierce features and low, agile hunting technique. Wheatears should be seen by the spoil heaps that remind the walker that they are passing through an area which used to be central to Arkengarthdale's lead mining industry. As Slei Gill narrows, you are in a prime place to see the rare ring ouzel in spring. They sometimes perch atop the wall bordering the path in April. This allows good views of a species that becomes much more elusive once it commences breeding. Stonechats can also be seen in the bracken areas on your left-hand side here and show well provided the wind isn't too strong.

🚶 **❸ Turn left onto the track and then follow it as it bends right through a gully (there is a shorter route that you can take that heads westwards along a path marked on the map but this is difficult to follow on the ground). Keep on the track to a junction**

Slei Gill – a good place to see ring ouzels in spring

at which you should bear left and descend on the path. Turn left onto an obvious stone track when reaching it and keep on this for a short distance until it veers left with a barn ahead. Here cross the stile visible on your right and head downhill keeping the wall just to your left. Ignore the left-hand path heading through the red gate and descend to another gate. Bear left down a gully between two walls and then bear right to join the lane. The lane then leads you back downhill to Langthwaite.

❶ Booze Moor is a real wilderness of heather-clad moorland and is at its best on a fine day. There are few of these in winter, though the determined birdwatcher visiting in these months might well encounter birds of prey. Buzzard, hen harrier and peregrine can all be anticipated at this time of year. Red grouse are still fairly common on the moor, where the habitat is carefully managed to provide maximum numbers for the 'Glorious Twelfth'. The first you might see of one is as it flies away uttering its typical 'goback' call, though they are sometimes quite approachable and obligingly visible on tracks or walls. The handsome golden plover breeds on the moor and the more elusive snipe can also be seen here. Curlews and lapwings feed in the fields as you descend towards Langthwaite. On the lane back down to the village look for linnets in the areas of bracken and spotted flycatchers in the bushes further down.

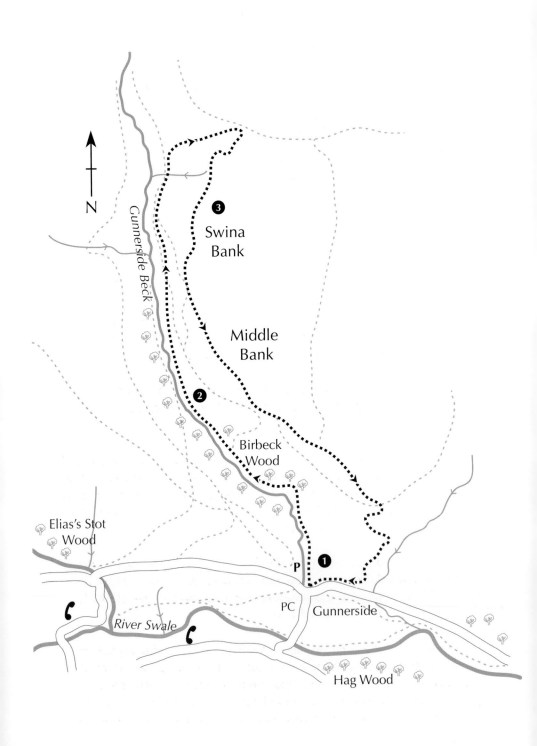

N

Gunnerside Beck

❸ Swina
Bank

Middle
Bank

❷

Birbeck
Wood

Elias's Stot
Wood

P ❶

PC Gunnerside

River Swale

Hag Wood

Gunnerside

Mines and ouzels up Gunnerside Gill

Ring ouzel

Length: 9 km (5.5 miles)
Time: 3 to 4 hours
Season: Late March to late July
Terrain/grade: Moderate
Start: Limited free parking in Gunnerside village by the bridge, SD951983
Bus/train: A bus service from Richmond run by Harkers, and Harrogate District Community Transport stops at Gunnerside Bridge (Monday to Saturday)
General: Pub and café in Gunnerside. For the public toilets take the first right after the bridge

THIS WALK COMBINES THE natural and social history of a fascinating area of Swaledale. The walk takes you through the remnants of Gunnerside's lead mining past whilst giving you as good a chance as anywhere in the country to see the scarce ring ouzel. The fine views across Swaledale on the return leg make this walk a captivating one throughout.

❶ Cross the bridge and take the first left to walk alongside the beck. Before the house follow the arrow leading you right up a set of steps. Follow the path along the east side of the gill as it takes you through the woodland.

The classic river birds of the Dales, the dipper and the grey wagtail, can both be seen on Gunnerside beck. House martins are present in good numbers in the village as they feed enthusiastically alongside swifts and swallows. Moving into the mixed woodland you will be struck by the rich ground flora, with carpets of bluebells and a few primroses and

117

wood anemones on show. Nuthatch and great spotted woodpecker can be seen here throughout the year. The portly build and the stunning red underparts of the male bullfinch make this species a particularly welcome sight. Sparrowhawks fly overhead with their characteristic flight pattern interspersed with frequent glides. Redpolls are typically unsettled as they move around the wood and their similarly attractive cousin, the siskin, can be seen throughout the year here.

❷ **Move out of the woodland, passing through two stiles and then keeping left by the drystone wall on the wide grassy path. Follow the wooden posts guiding the way through the spoil heaps and then climb on the track up towards Middle Bank. Continue on this track past the Bunton Mines and then uphill slightly to reach a couple of cairns and a 4-waymarker post. At the post follow the right-hand sign for Surrender Bridge. Take the clear path here, almost doubling back on yourself uphill, and follow it until you reach a set of spoil heaps above the stream.**

ⓘ Once past the woodland you are entering an area that was once the heart of a bustling lead mining industry. Lead mining dominated the local area from the late seventeenth century, though it declined fairly rapidly in the nineteenth century. A sign on your right points out where the lead was 'dressed', a term used to describe the separation of the ore from the waste minerals. An old rusty tank on your left as you climb towards Middle Bank was the compression chamber for the Sir Francis Mine. By the end of the nineteenth century it was possible to disappear underground in Gunnerside Gill and surface 11.3 km (7 miles) away in Arkengarthdale (Walk 25)! Work was desperately hard for the miners, though, with industrial accidents and disease commonplace. The smelters further up the ghyll at Blakethwaite had it even worse, with an average life expectancy of about 35 in the mid nineteenth century.

Now the area is splendidly tranquil and dominated only by our 'mountain black bird', the ring ouzel. There are a number of pairs of this appealing bird in the area and you should look out for them from Middle Bank onwards. Listen for its loud clicking call and check the walls and the scars around Swina Bank. Good views should hopefully be obtained of the white chest crescent and pale wing panel. Ouzels are present in the area from the end of March until late July at least, though they can be elusive in the summer months. An April visit is ideal and sees them at their most showy before they become shy and retiring when breeding. The heart of ring ouzel country around

Bunton Hush combines birdwatching and history perfectly. The 'hushes' are named after the early technique of hushing, where water was dammed up and then released in an attempt to expose the lead ore. Unsurprisingly, severe flooding downstream could often result from this technique and it was eventually prohibited. The ouzels have, however, taken happily to the rocky gills formed by the process.

❸ The next section can be difficult to follow from the map and this route is recommended, though it is not the shortest way back. At the spoil heaps the path becomes difficult to discern but you can follow a faint path which bears left uphill at about 10 o'clock and takes you to a crumbling drystone wall. Follow the wall up to a clear track and turn right onto this. Keep on this track as other paths join it, heading through a wooden gate and then on past a series of barns and houses on your right. Pass the scars on your left and then take the track heading right which is marked as a minor road on the OS map. Ignoring the footpath on your left leading to Low Row, skirt left along a faint path by the drystone wall to cut off the corner and join the track heading east. Before you reach a house on your left, turn right downhill and take the path sandwiched between two drystone walls. When you cross the stream and pass a barn on your left, veer left with the drystone wall to reach an obvious track which you then turn right onto. This joins a lane and you then pass through a small wooden gate back to the village.

The long wings and powerful flight of the raven are an impressive sight towards the top end of the gill. A few pairs of merlin breed in the general area and one might be seen dashing low over the moor. As you climb up towards the heather tops the red grouse, the emblematic bird of the moors, can be seen all year round. Heading along the ridge the flashing white rump of the wheatear is a common sight. Wheatears appeared to have declined in many areas of the Dales but it is still possible to become blasé about them on this walk as they seem to be everywhere. The ridge can be good for raptors that use the updraft from the westerly wind. A winter or early spring visit might produce a peregrine, buzzard or hen harrier. The views across Swaledale here are superb and on a fine day it is difficult to resist stopping to revel in the scenery. As you return to the village listen out for the yaffle of the green woodpecker and look for the dumpy shape of a little owl perched on the wall. If your timing is impeccable and your luck is in, an osprey will cruise over the Swale to round off a perfect walk.

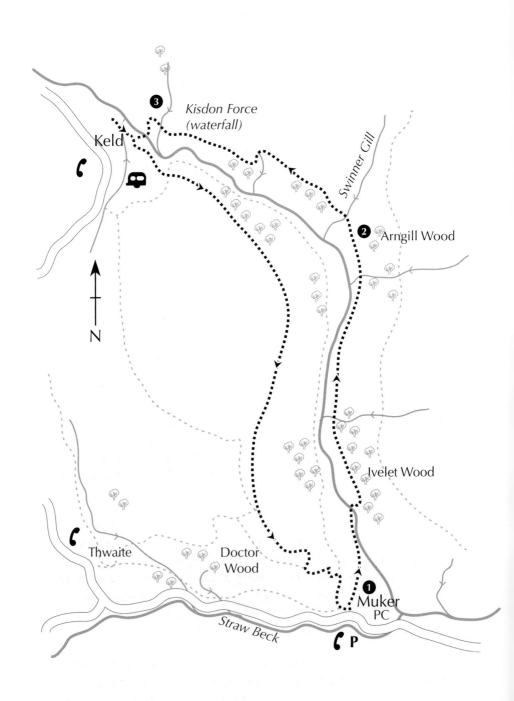

Kisdon Force
(waterfall)

❸

Keld

Swinner Gill

❷ Arngill Wood

N

Ivelet Wood

Thwaite

Doctor
Wood

❶
Muker
PC

Straw Beck

P

Muker

The raven and the best of Swaledale

Raven

Length: 9.5 km (5.5 miles)
Time: Allow 4 hours
Season: March to August
Terrain/grade: Moderate
Start: There is plenty of parking in Muker, SD909978
Bus/train: Buses run by Harkers, and Harrogate District Community Transport from Richmond west across Swaledale stop at Muker bus stop in the centre of the village (Monday to Saturday)
General: Cafés, pubs and public toilets in Muker

THIS IS A FABULOUS walk irrespective of birds, but fortunately the birdlife lives up to the scenery in this circular of Upper Swaledale. From the stroll alongside the clear waters of the Swale to the climb up the side of Kisdon Hill to look across to the ridges where the raven glides, this is a walk which is sure to delight.

❶ **In the village take the lane in the centre leading up the hill past the benches. At the top of the incline take the footpath signed Gunnerside and Keld off to your right which takes you through the meadows. Please keep single file to the paved path here. On reaching the river turn right at the 3-way signpost marked Gunnerside. Cross the bridge and then take a left onto a stone track which you follow up the valley.**

ⓘ The meadows between Muker and the Swale are full of wild flowers in the summer and are beautiful to wander through. House martins and swallows skim low searching for insects, whilst spotted flycatchers perch on fences bordering the meadows. With such a profusion of grasses and flowers it can be difficult to pick out different species but look for pignut, wood crane's bill and even melancholy thistle. Reaching the Swale gives a taste of the scenery to come and also a chance to see the special river birds of the Dales. Grey wagtail and dipper are regular sights whilst common sandpiper and oystercatcher make sure things are never quiet in the summer. The kingfisher roams up the Swale to here and can be seen downstream of the bridge or perched on rocks upstream. The wooded hillsides throughout this section of the walk hold the handsome redstart in the breeding season. Nuthatches can be seen throughout the year and tree pipits sing in spring in the more sparsely wooded areas with plenty of bracken.

(🚶) ❷ **At the bridge over the stream make sure you take the track straight ahead heading uphill through a wooden gate. Continue for another kilometre and a half (about a mile) before crossing a stream, then take the path left signed the Pennine Way.**

ⓘ The raven has had such a troubled past in the Dales that it is truly heartwarming to see the bird battle against the odds to soar above Swaledale once again. Ravens were persecuted to near extinction by the turn of the twentieth century by gamekeepers and egg collectors. They still face persecution today but thankfully the section of the walk from the bridge over East Gill beck to Kisdon Hill provides a chance to see this majestic bird. Ravens might be difficult to separate on the ground at a distance from the crow but in flight they cut a distinct and imposing sight. They seem to use hardly any energy, slowly beating their buzzard-sized wings yet moving at speed with a thick outstretched neck and a characteristic diamond-shaped tail. Make sure you are also alert for the more elusive ring ouzel, particularly around Swinner Gill in spring. If birding seems good here now, though, think what it must have been like in the distant past. Arn was the Norse name for Golden Eagle and with Arngill Wood, Arn Gill and Arn Gill Head all still on the OS map of the area today it is fair to assume that eagles must have patrolled the ridges here once. When watching a raven, peregrine or buzzard over Swinner Gill imagine a bird with nearly twice the wingspan alongside them. Competition for prime crag nesting sites must have been fierce!

⊛ ❸ **Cross the bridge over the Swale and continue up the hill. Turn left at the top, signed Thwaite/Muker. Stay on the Pennine Way, detouring left to Kisdon Force and then retracing your steps if you want to see the waterfall. Follow the Pennine Way signs whenever the path splits until you begin to descend down towards Muker. With a barn to your left take the left-hand bridleway signed Muker (when the Pennine Way veers off right). Continue on this stone track back to the top of the village.**

ⓘ Pause at the bridge to check for kingfisher, dipper and grey wagtail before climbing up to take the path along the side of Kisdon Hill. The path takes you through woodland, which is excellent for redstart and spotted flycatcher. Look for redpolls and siskins moving busily around below and listen for the song of the tree pipit. Roe deer can be seen here occasionally and the path makes a good vantage point, from which to look for birds of prey. Peregrine, buzzard, kestrel and sparrowhawk might all be seen at any time of the year. Descending back down into Muker the views are superb as the skylarks and meadow pipits serenade you home.

Ring ouzel

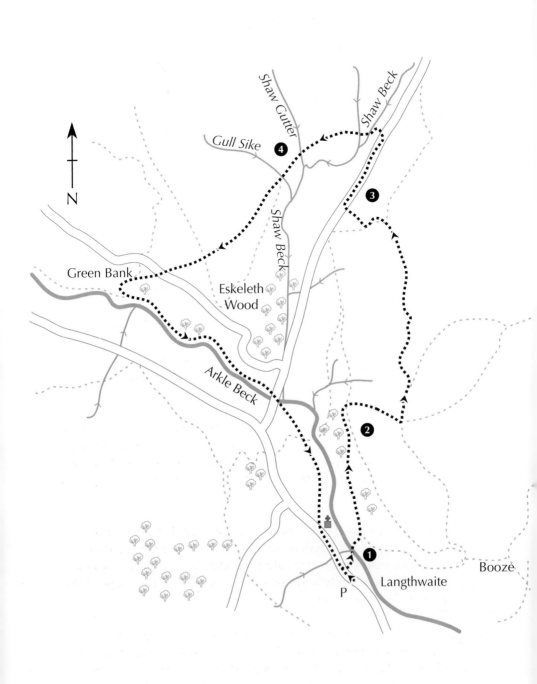

Shaw Gutter

Shaw Beck

Gull Sike

4

3

Shaw Beck

N

Green Bank

Eskeleth
Wood

Arkle Beck

2

1

Booze

P

Langthwaite

Langthwaite

Black grouse and Arkengarthdale

Black grouse

Length: Around 10 km (6 miles)

Time: Allow 4 hours

Season: All year, though the grouse are difficult to see in the summer months from late June to August

Terrain/grade: Moderate

Start: Langthwaite pay and display car park, NZ005024

Bus/train: None currently available – nearest bus stop is in Reeth

General: Refreshments at the Red Lion, Langthwaite
Toilet block in the village north of the car park

THIS CIRCULAR WALK AROUND remote and sparsely populated Arkengarthdale takes you through the heart of black grouse country. The dale is an escape from the bustle of the busy tourist-orientated areas at the weekend. In place of people there are plenty of birds and superbly characterful turkey-sized grouse!

❶ **Turn right out of the car park and take the first lane right. Cross the bridge and continue on the lane uphill past the Red Lion. As the road bends right sharply take the bridleway signed on your left. Follow this path as it takes you along the edge of the wood and then veers uphill.**

ⓘ As you enter Scar House woods the rich birdlife of the walk is immediately apparent. In winter there are great spotted woodpeckers and flocks of fieldfare but it is in spring that the woods really come alive. Spotted flycatchers arrive and busily hunt for insects from branches, and willow warblers establish their territory with equal gusto. The woods are an excellent place to see the attractive figure of the male redstart. Redstarts can be seen in the scattered bushes on your left as you skirt the bottom of the wood and, particularly, in the bushes before you turn right and ascend the hillside. Your eyes need to work overtime here as common blue butterflies skim across the path and buzzards soar overhead in their effortless fashion.

(🕅) ❷ **Come out onto the grassy path above the wood and take the first right signed up the hillside. Follow the small waymarker posts up the hillside and then turn left onto a stony track. Follow this track, bearing left when it forks after around 200 m (220 yards). Keep on the stone track as it decends to the road.**

❶ As you move away from the woods be alert for raptors as they use the updraft from westerly winds to hunt the ridge. Peregrines are regular here in the winter months and the pulse will quicken should you be lucky enough to see a female hen harrier. Keep an eye out for the powerful figure of the raven as it glides over the ridge. Wheatears arrive in late March and can be seen well as they stand boldly upright.

(🕅) ❸ **Turn right onto the road and continue on it before taking the track on your left just past the farm. Pass over the small bridge and then bear right by the sign for a public bridleway. Pass through the gate and keep left near the wall to a metal gate. Keep right by the wall to another gate and then keep right by the fence, taking care crossing a small stream.**

❶ Birdwatchers cannot help but love the eccentric black grouse. The hillside above Shaw Farm provides a superb chance to see this species. Male black grouse, known as blackcock, have broad red eyebrows and an attractive blueish gloss to their plumage when seen well. Their tubby frame, weighing in at around two kilos (just over four pounds), makes them something of a weird and wonderful sight as they gather on the pastures of Arkengarthdale. When you reach the road, look across the valley to the fields around some ruined barns opposite. The sedentary grouse are usually present but the early spring is best. Take care to keep to the footpath as you pass across the hillside so as not to disturb these scarce birds. Sympathetic management of the east Arkengarthdale common has allowed the black grouse to make a welcome comeback here towards the southernmost edge of its range in England.

View across Arkengarthdale from Green Bank:
the dale is a stronghold of the rare black grouse

This is a terrific place for birdwatching in general, with many wading birds finding the area to their liking. Snipe engage in their extraordinary drumming display in the spring, where the bleating noise is made by the air rushing through their tail feathers as they descend. Redshank, lapwing and curlew nest in the pastures and golden plover gather in large numbers alongside the grouse in the spring. Look along the road to the east, where short-eared owls can be seen quartering. The merlin can be seen hunting low over the horizon in the breeding season. Grey wagtails inhabit the small stream whilst two birds in national decline, the grey partridge and the skylark, still thrive in the area.

❹ Keep on the visible path as it passes over boggy ground and then descends with drystone walls on your left and bracken on your right. Bear right on the track taking you out onto the road and turn right onto this. Continue for around 400 m (440 yards) before seeing a footpath sign on your right-hand side. Opposite this on your left is a stone track descending downhill (note this is not clear on the OS map). Take this and pass through the metal gate straight ahead (not the one on your left). Bear right along

Juvenille spotted flycatcher, Eskeleth Bridge, July 2007

a wall for a short while and then turn left and pass through a gap in the wall to the left of the house. Head towards the fence bordering a young woodland and descend downhill, passing through a gap in the wall below. A faint path then takes you the short distance to the main path along the river. Turn left onto this and continue on it towards Eskeleth Bridge. In the last field before the bridge bear right over a wooden footbridge and head left along the river to the road. Cross the road onto the track (signed footpath only). Continue on the track, cutting right through a gap in the wall by the houses and rejoining the track leading along to the church. Turn left after the church and follow the pavement back to the car park.

i As you descend towards the road check the fields to your left where you can often see hares at close range. They can be seen boxing in the spring when the female vigorously fends off the unwanted attentions of the male. The areas of bracken to your right are the haunt of the attractive linnet whilst the young woodland on your left as you descend to Green Bank holds its pretty cousin, the redpoll. The walk back along the river takes you through woodland home to the pied flycatcher in the spring and nuthatch throughout the year. Pause to look at the river between the footbridge and Eskeleth Bridge as this is a reliable place for dippers. Bramblings gather in flocks here in the winter and spotted flycatchers sometimes perch on the bridge itself in the spring and summer months.

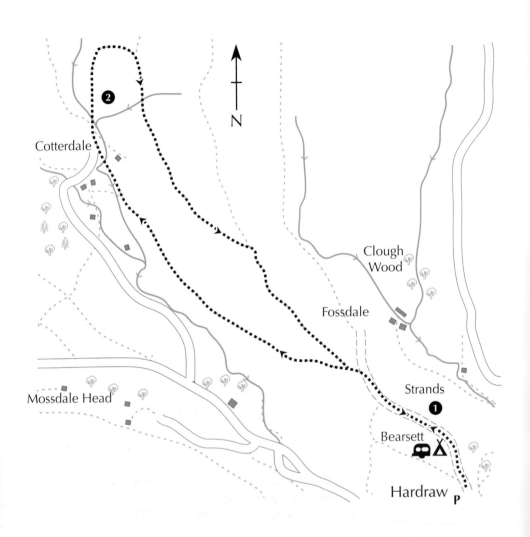

Cotterdale

Clough
Wood

Fossdale

Mossdale Head

Strands

Bearsett

Hardraw P

Hardraw

The return of the buzzard to Wensleydale

Buzzard

Length: 10 km (6 miles)
Time: Allow 4 hours
Season: April to August
Terrain/grade: Moderate/Challenging
Start: Hardraw village, please park carefully at the
side of the road west of the village, SD867912
Bus/train: None currently available
General: Refreshments in Hardraw village

WENSLEYDALE IS RIGHTLY A popular place, with tourist crowds flocking to Hawes in the summer months. This walk escapes the crowds a few miles away and takes you up to the secluded hamlet of Cotterdale, providing splendid views across Upper Wensleydale in the process. The welcome return of the buzzard can be witnessed as it glides on the thermals at the head of the valley.

❶ Take the Pennine Way heading north at the western edge of the village. Follow this lane up the hillside for about 1.6 km (1 mile). Shortly after a right turn signed for Pickersett Nab, turn left off the Pennine Way on the path signed for Cotterdale. Follow this path as it skirts the hillside and begins to descend to the hamlet. Ignore the stile and signs downhill to your left and follow the path roughly along the line of telegraph poles. Take the footbridge over the beck.

❶ In Hardraw village don't miss the chance to see England's highest single-drop waterfall, Hardraw Force. Entry is through the Green Dragon pub where a small admission charge is payable. After wet weather the force is particularly impressive, as William Wordsworth noted after his late eighteenth-century visit. Wordsworth braved a 'mountain storm' to visit the waterfall and for once found words difficult to come by to describe the dramatic scene. Heading through the village onto the Pennine Way you are likely to be greeted by the chirpings of house sparrows and the pleasant notes of the goldfinch. Check the first wooded area on your left-hand side for the spotted flycatchers which arrive in May. The ascent heading towards Great Shunner Fell is wearing and it becomes easy to see why the fell is so dreaded by Pennine Way walkers. The skylark should help you along with its famous song, and a sighting of one skulking in the grass with its crest erected is possible.

Skirting the hillside into the small valley of Cotterdale the walking becomes easier and the birds more plentiful. Wheatears are numerous on the hillside in the spring and summer. They will often perch boldly on drystone walls and rocks allowing close study of their neat plumage. Stonechats join them and further down towards the valley bottom the curlew and lapwing compete with the oystercatcher for the title of most often-heard wader. As you descend, the small areas of bushes and trees hold redstarts and a few redpoll, whilst the rushy areas are the home of the reed bunting.

The hamlet you reach shares the same name as the valley and has a history stretching back over two thousand years. Little is known about the early settlers here but an excellently preserved Iron Age sword can be found at the British Museum. By the time of the 1603 census Cotterdale had become a place of refuge for six wealthy men who are thought to be relatives of Catholics involved in plots against the Protestant Queen Elizabeth I. You can see why it was chosen given its remote setting, with the few remaining residents now surrounded by wildlife. Hares can be found in the fields and the occasional wily fox might be encountered. The village itself plays host to many birds, with the great spotted woodpecker climbing the tree trunks and the blackcap singing from the bushes. At the entrance to the forest you will see a sign explaining the High Abbotside regeneration project. This is aimed at creating a heather grouse moor and helping black grouse build their numbers up in the area. Black grouse can sometimes be seen in the fields near the village or on the slopes of Great Shunner Fell from the Pennine Way.

⊛ ❷ **Continue through the village past the last house and then take the second bridge on your right. Follow the track as it zigzags up through the conifers. There are numerous tracks leading off here so follow the public bridleway signs that guide you through. Once out of the forest bear right along the track skirting the edge**

of the conifers. Rejoin the Pennine Way and turn right downhill, signed for Hardraw, with a stile soon after you take the turn. Return downhill back to Hardraw.

ⓘ Climbing through the dark forest, birds become more difficult to see, though goldcrests are present in good numbers. Once out of the conifers and heading along the hillside you have a good chance of seeing a buzzard. The buzzard was reportedly very common in Wensleydale in the mid nineteenth century but only a century later the decimation of the rabbit population by myxomatosis had taken its toll and the few pairs in the Dales were restricted to the Howgills. Now the buzzard has returned and can be seen again in Wensleydale. You have the rare opportunity here to look down on birds of prey hunting the hillside, though on a fine day the buzzard might still soar on thermals above you. Its broad wings are held in a characteristic V shape when soaring and the underwing shows a variegated plumage, including a pale band across the chest. Other birds of prey also thrive here, with the sparrowhawk a regular sight as it flashes across the hillside terrorising the wheatears, and family parties of kestrels hovering nearby in the summer. Crows gather on the slopes and the raven is a frequent sight with its powerful flight and rolling calls.

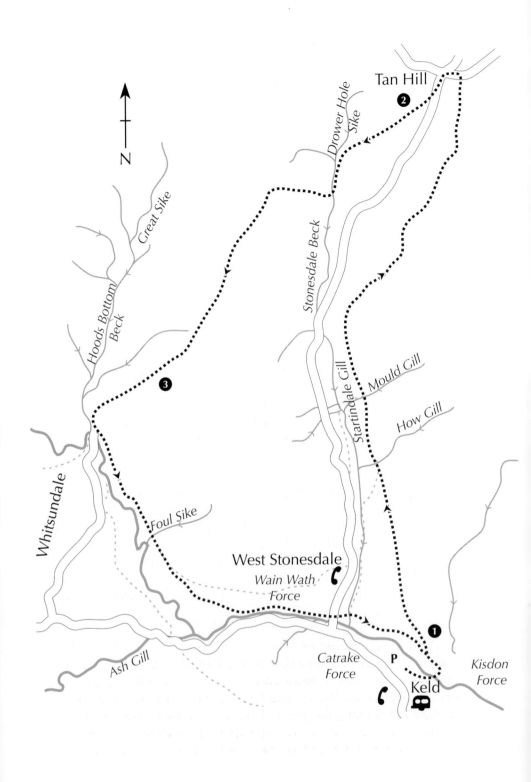

N

Great Sike

Hoods Bottom Beck

Drower Hole Sike

Tan Hill

❷

Stonesdale Beck

Mould Gill

How Gill

Startindale Gill

❸

Whitsundale

Foul Sike

West Stonesdale

Wain Wath Force

❶

Ash Gill

Catrake Force

P

Keld

Kisdon Force

Keld

To Tan Hill with the golden plover

Golden plover

Length: 16 km (10 miles)
Time: Allow 7 hours
Season: April to July
Terrain/grade: Moderate/Challenging
Start: Car park at Park Lodge, Keld, NY892013. Small fee payable by honesty box
Bus/train: Buses run by Harkers and Harrogate District Community Transport from Richmond west across Swaledale stop by the turn off from the B6270 to Keld (Monday to Saturday)
General: Tan Hill Inn. Light refreshments available in Keld village. Toilet block in Keld, NY893012

T HIS IS A WALK through a ruggedly attractive area of the Dales with an optional stop en route at Britain's highest public house, the isolated Tan Hill Inn. It is difficult not to be struck by the wonderful variety of scenery and wildlife on this walk. It starts with pretty Keld and its waterfalls before moving on to the wilderness of Stonesdale moor and then returns via the delightfully tranquil valley of Whitsundale. There are all the special upland birds of the Dales and you have a good chance of seeing the beautiful breeding plumage of the golden plover.

❶ **Head out of the car park on the path signed to Muker. After a short while turn left downhill on the Pennine Way and cross the bridge over the Swale. Head up the hill and turn left onto the Pennine Way above the waterfall. On reaching the farmyard head straight uphill along the grassy track to a wooden gate. Keep on the path ahead when you are walking through the area of pasture. There will be a barn on your left and a track leading left**

but keep straight ahead on the grassy path leading to a gate. The Pennine Way is then fairly easy to follow as you head uphill after Lad Gill and then on to Tan Hill (bear left as signposted).

🛈 Keld is a popular base for walking excursions as the Coast to Coast long distance path and the Pennine Way cross here. It is, however, rarely visited by birdwatchers despite being excellent for birds in the spring and summer. Heading towards the River Swale look for redpoll and spotted flycatcher in the trees and bushes lining the path. Dipper, kingfisher and grey wagtail are all possible on the river as you cross over the bridge. The curious might want to make a small detour along to Kisdon Force, though the pleasant Catrake Force can be seen before you head uphill on the Pennine Way.

As you move up towards the wild expanse of Stonesdale Moor, the birdlife changes with the scenery. The curlew gives its familiar call whilst meadow pipits abound in this habitat. As you move beyond West Stonesdale in the valley below, you reach an area of improved pasture with scattered barns. This is a good place to look for the chunky frame and distinct plumage of the male black grouse.

Black grouse

As you head towards Tan Hill, the past importance of coal mining to the area is still visible in the landscape. Coal, albeit of a poor quality, was mined here from at least the twelfth century. It later became tied up with the lead mining industry as the coal was converted to coke to be used in lead smelting at Old Gang and Gunnerside (Walk 26). The area is now the home of the golden plover which arrives in April. The somewhat melancholy whistle of the plover can be heard as you approach the pub. The real aim of the birdwatcher, though, must be to see the dazzling summer plumage of this wader. The upperpart feathers of the plover are edged with a rich gold colour that makes the return of this wader to the Dales a welcome and beautiful sight.

❷ **Head west on the road alongside the pub and take the minor road left to West Stonesdale. After a short distance take the path right signed to Ravenseat. The path is reasonably well signposted though fairly faint as it crosses a stream and then heads uphill alongside a gill. Bear left at the brow of the hill as signposted. The path then becomes less easy to follow. There are two options here, you can try and keep on the path itself, which keeps fairly level and cuts directly across to a gap in the fence. A longer option, more straightforward in terms of navigation, is to bear right along an initially visible track which skirts the hillside of Robert's Seat. This will take you to a fence which you can then follow down to the signposted gap.**

Tan Hill Inn comes highly recommended as a very convenient stop nearly halfway through this walk. This is Britain's highest pub, standing at 528 m (1,732 feet) above sea level, and the warmth of the coal fire here has provided welcome relief for many a walker over the years. The pub stands just inside North Yorkshire and has been featured on television many times. Tan Hill has had to cope with its fair share of adversity down the years, with the closure of the mines and the extremes of the weather, though an expected battle occurred recently with Kentucky Fried Chicken when the company claimed a copyright infringement by the pub because its annual Christmas dinner was termed a 'family feast'! Fortunately a robust response lead to the fast food giant being forced to back down in its proceedings against the humble Tan Hill Inn.

It is a wonder so much birdlife survives the changeable and harsh weather around Tan Hill but in fact the area has excellent potential for the birdwatcher. Birds are few and far between in the winter months though perseverance could be rewarded with a hen harrier, raven, or even a snow bunting. Spring brings the short-eared owls that are best looked for at dawn or dusk. Heading towards Whitsundale, with the gentle peaks of Thomas Gill Hill and Robert's Seat to your right, you have another chance to acquaint yourself with the golden plover whilst skylarks perform their song flight noisily above. The merlin is a regular sight in this area as it hunts low over the moorland looking to pounce on an unfortunate meadow pipit.

(🚶) ❸ **Begin the descent to Whitsundale, following a gill with a fence to your left. Before reaching Whitsundale Beck you need to turn left through a metal gate. This takes you through the field and out with a house to your left. Continue straight on a wide grassy path signed to Keld and follow this as it skirts the hillside, bearing right along the more obvious track at Oven Mouth.**

🛈 Whitsundale is a hidden gem, with its inaccessibility meaning few tourists get to appreciate the clear waters of Whitsundale Beck as it flows down through the steep gorge of How Edge Scars. As you descend to Whitsundale the fields are full of wading birds in the spring and summer with lapwing and curlew abounding. Snipe breed in the areas of rushes whilst oystercatchers inject noise and colour into a peaceful scene. As you skirt the hillside above the beck keep an eye out for our mountain blackbird, the ring ouzel, which frequents Whitsundale in the spring and summer months. Kestrels patrol the hillside on your return to Keld and those eager for more natural beauty can make a short detour to see Wainwath Falls and its faithful dippers and grey wagtails.

Bibliography and further reading

Ralph Chislett, *Yorkshire Birds* (1952)

Ian Court, *Birds of Conservation Concern in the Yorkshire Dales National Park* (2000)

John R.Mather, *Birds of Yorkshire* (1986)

W.R.Mitchell, *Birds of the Yorkshire Dales* (1998)

T.H.Nelson, *The Birds of Yorkshire* (1907)

Peter Wright, *Merlins of the South-East Yorkshire Dales* (2005)

Birdwatching/Walking Notes

Birdwatching/Walking Notes

Birdwatching/Walking Notes